Ex Libris

K

Kay E. Lindquist

Artist

Greeting Card
DESIGN

Greeting Card DESIGN

Joanne Fink

GRAPHIC *details*

An Imprint of

PBC INTERNATIONAL, INC.

Distributor to the book trade in the United States and Canada:
Rizzoli International Publications Inc.
300 Park Avenue South
New York, NY 10010

Distributor to the art trade in the United States and Canada:
PBC International, Inc.
One School Street
Glen Cove, NY 11542
1-800-527-2826
Fax 516-676-2738

Distributor throughout the rest of the world:
Hearst Books International
1350 Avenue of the Americas
New York, NY 10019

Library of Congress Cataloging-in-Publication Data

Greeting card design / by Joanne Fink.
        p.   cm.
Includes index.
ISBN 0-86636-182-0
1. Greeting cards--United States. I. Title.
NC1856.F56   1992
741.6′84′0973--dc20   92-1071
                                                                        CIP

CAVEAT—Extensive research has gone into the creation of this book.
Credit information on each card was supplied by the card's publisher.
The author has made every effort to insure the accuracy of
this manuscript.

Hand lettered chapter headings
by Judy Kastin

Color separation, printing and binding by
Toppan Printing Co. (H.K.) Ltd. Hong Kong

Typography by
TypeLink, Inc.

10 9 8 7 6 5 4 3 2 1

Christmas
Birthday
Valentine's Day
Anniversary
Mother's Day
Father's Day
Graduation
Halloween
Hanukkah
Die Cut

Dedication

*For my family with love,
and my friends, Janet Hoffberg and Judy Kastin, with thanks.*

Baby
Blank
Easter
Encouragement
Congratulations
Get Well
Romantic Love
Religious
Sympathy
Friendship
Wedding
Photographic
Juvenile
Three Dimensional
Lettering
Gift Cards
Louie Awards
Gift Enclosures
Handmade

TABLE OF CONTENTS

It seems fitting that a book about the U.S. greeting card industry should arrive in 1992, the year that marks the culmination of the European Economic Community initiative. Ours is a mature industry—albeit thriving at $5 billion in U.S. retail sales for 1991—and so we may need to look outside our own borders for growth opportunities. Naturally we observe the activity of the European Common Market with rising expectations.

But readers who would look for predictions about how the EEC initiative will play out for U.S. greeting card exporters will have to look elsewhere. The dizzying pace and stunning nature of the events throughout Europe and the former Soviet Union certainly convinced this would-be fortune-teller to wait and see.

Right now, the European card market is dominated by a few large firms with the resources to meet the challenges of exporting. If the EEC initiative makes it less cumbersome and less expensive to negotiate sales through the ability to use a single European distributor, smaller companies may find it practical and profitable to enter the export market and the volume of European card sales by American firms will likely grow.

FOREWORD

Back home, there are a host of demographic and social trends that are influencing the greeting card industry. In the Greeting Card Association, we've identified a number of trends for which our members have created special product lines. The so-called graying of America—the growing number of seniors—has produced a market for cards that reflect the interests of older people. Subjects range from health issues to congratulations on becoming a great-grandparent. The increase in the number of working women has created a market for messages about office politics, juggling career and family, and so forth. The national obsession with dieting, health and fitness has spawned a host of cards that poke fun at the pain of self-denial. Responding to the high divorce rate, there are cards on the market that may help friends offer support for a couple splitting up.

Other trends reflected on the greeting card shelves include a revival of romance and traditional values. Friendship cards have grown in popularity. There are cards from parent to child and cards that transcend "get well" to address the realities of terminal illness.

What about the future of our industry in an age of instantaneous communication: Where does the greeting card fit in among the faxes, the cellular phone calls and the E-mail? A look back may help put things in perspective. In the early years of this century, as Ford cranked his assembly line, the Wright brothers took off from Kitty Hawk, the first transatlantic radio telegraph transmitted and the first newsreels fascinated moviegoers, greeting card pioneers American Greetings, Rust Craft, Hallmark, Norcross and my own grandfather opened shop. Had they been daunted by the swift progress of communications and other technology, our industry wouldn't be where it is today.

Who can predict what tomorrow may bring? I'd like to think that no matter how much things change, the ink-and-paper greeting card will remain a tangible way to express our sentiments. So it's a good time for a book like this to showcase some of the best our industry has produced over the last few years.

James F. Burgoyne
President
Greeting Card Associaton

Greeting cards touch so many lives; they are a form of communication used to express a complete range of positive emotions: such as love, romance, joy, encouragement, appreciation, friendship and caring. Although the exact origin of the greeting card has been lost in antiquity, it is possible to trace its development to early Egyptian and Chinese civilizations. The Egyptians exchanged greetings on colorfully decorated papyrus scrolls, and the Chinese celebrated the New Year with written messages of good will. These customs were the forebears of the modern greeting card.

The earliest known card was printed as a New Year's greeting in Rhine, Germany, in 1450. Valentine's Day, the first holiday when people exchanged cards, began to be celebrated with written messages around that same time. In 1843 the first Christmas card was designed by John Calcott Horsley, at the request of Sir Henry Cole. Exchanging cards that contained good wishes for the holiday season quickly become a popular custom in Europe. It was not long after, that the American card industry was born.

The history of the American greeting card industry revolves around Louis Prang, known today as the "Father of the American Greeting Card." A German emigrant to Boston, Prang founded a small lithography business in 1856, and by 1866 perfected the lithographic process to the point that even experts had difficulty differentiating his prints from the original art. In 1874 he combined his lithographic techniques with printed sentiments to create a line of Christmas cards, which he offered in England. The success of his cards in England convinced Prang to offer them in America the following year.

Christmas cards had been available in America since the 1840's, but they were not mass produced until Prang offered his deluxe line in 1875. Five years later these cards were so popular that Prang had to employ 300 workers in order to keep up with public demand. In addition to Christmas cards, he also published cards for New Year, Birthdays and Easter. By 1890, inexpensive German imports flooded the American market, causing Prang to abandon his greeting card publishing business for other concerns. The Louie Awards, given annually by the Greeting Card Association in recognition of excellence and creativity in the industry, are named for Louis Prang.

INTRODUCTION

Louis Prang cards
circa 1880s
Courtesy of Frank LoCicero

The period between 1890 and 1906 was not an active one in the history of the industry. In the early 1900's however, with the establishment of several major firms, including Hallmark and American Greetings, the industry began to grow. During World War I sales of greeting cards quadrupled, and by 1919 cards were an established part of American life. The Great Depression that hurt so many American businesses actually caused the greeting card industry to flourish, as people substituted cards for gifts they could not afford. The depression ended with World War II, and the greeting card business became a major American industry.

In the mid 1950's, small companies appeared on the scene and offered alternatives to the traditional cards published by existing major companies. Known as Studio Cards, these risque and often insulting cards were extremely popular with the younger generation. The large companies realized the potential of this new genre, and came out with their own similiar lines.

By the 1960's "informals"—cute cards with simple designs and short sentiments—were introduced, and outsold traditional offerings by as much as three to one. The early 1970's saw two introductions that were both successful: "Soft-Touch Cards" and "Alternative Cards." Soft-Touch cards combined romantic, photographic images with expressive verse, while Alternative cards offered an offbeat, humorous but sensitive approach to everyday situations. Humor began to play a larger role in the card market, becoming one of the best selling categories.

The alternative card market expanded tremendously in the early 1980's, and in 1985 the big three of Hallmark, American Greetings and Gibson, entered the alternative card market, causing many smaller companies to fold. New companies continued to spring up; in fact, the number of greeting card companies grew tremendously during this period. By the early 1990's there were over 1,000 greeting card publishers, ranging from major corporations to small family run operations.

The late 1980's and early 1990's saw various changes in the industry. As consumers became more aware of environmental issues, card companies responded by printing more cards on recycled stock. Distribution channels changed, with more cards being sold through supermarkets and drugstores than ever before. Cards focusing on the growing Juvenile market became prevalent; Encouragement cards, and other cards that could be sent at any time, became commonplace. The industry continued to grow, and in 1991 sales passed the $5 billion mark.

1991 also marked the 50th anniversary of the Greeting Card Association. Based in Washington, D.C., the GCA is the only trade organization to represent the industry. Their approximately 150 member companies produce over 90 percent of the greeting cards marketed annually in the United States. In addition to acting as an industry advocate, and serving as a resource center, the GCA represents industry interests before federal legislative and regulatory bodies, and promotes the tradition of sending greeting cards.

The GCA was instrumental in establishing the Greeting Card Creative Network. Headquartered in Washington, D.C., the GCCN is an organization that works to promote relations between publishers and the designers and writers who freelance in the stationery industry. Founded in 1988, the growing membership is comprised mostly of artists and other creative individuals.

Greeting cards play a significant role in American life. A greeting card is often sent instead of a letter. People who have difficulty expressing their feelings frequently allow a greeting card to speak for them. Greeting cards are also tangible substitutes for phone calls or visits. They help people stay in touch. The message in a greeting card is of supreme importance to the sender; it must convey the sender's thoughts and feelings in a warm, personal manner. A successful greeting card clearly expresses the relationship of the sender to the recipient—greeting card publishers refer to this as a "me-to-you-message"—and also conveys the feeling or mood of the sending occasion.

The message of a greeting card is communicated by both the design and the verse, and how they interact. The design attracts the consumer to the card, but it is the verse that causes the customer to either purchase the card, or return it to the rack and search for one that better expresses what he or she wants to say.

Greeting cards are used all over the world, but are especially popular in the United States. In 1991 Americans exchanged more than 7.8 billion greeting cards; the average American receives 31 cards each year. Counter cards, individual cards sold from a rack, range in price from $.35 to $7.50, with the average card costing $1.50. It is estimated that 85 to 90 percent of all greeting cards are purchased by women. The median age of a card buyer is 47 years old.

COMPANIES

In order to gain a more complete understanding of the greeting card industry, it is important to know something about the history of its major players. The big three—Hallmark, American Greetings and Gibson together comprise more than 85 percent of the market. They are also among the oldest greeting card companies still in existence.

HALLMARK

Hallmark Cards, Inc., the largest and best known of all card companies was founded in 1910 by 18-year-old Joyce C. Hall. Hall grew up in Nebraska, and became fascinated with picture postcards when a traveling salesman brought them into his family's store. Postcards, mostly imported from Germany, were in vogue in the early 1900's, and were avidly collected for their bright pictures.

At the tender age of 16, Hall convinced his two older brothers, Rollie and Bill, to join him in forming the "Norfolk Post Card Company." Two years later he moved the business to Kansas City, where he sold postcards from his room at the YMCA.

Despite the public's continuing interest in collecting postcards, Hall felt that they were not as good a means of communication between people as greeting cards were. Therefore, he decided to concentrate his marketing efforts on greeting cards, and by 1915 the Halls were publishing cards for Christmas, Valentine's Day and Birthdays. In 1919, they added Friendship cards to their inventory. The company's name was changed to Hall Brothers and in 1954 it was renamed Hallmark Cards, Inc.

The driving creative force behind Hallmark's success, Hall personally approved every new greeting card design until he was in his late seventies. In 1982, at the age of 91, Joyce Hall died. His vision is carried on by his son, Donald Joyce Hall, the current Chairman of the Board. Hallmark is a privately held company; the family owns 67 percent of the stock, and the employees hold the rest.

Hallmark and their subsidiary, Ambassador, publish more than 11 million greeting cards and 1.5 million related products each working day. Their cards and other products are published in over 20 languages and distributed in more than 100 countries. According to Hallmark, annual sales exceeded 2.7 billion dollars in 1991, giving it a domestic market share of around 45 percent.

Headquartered in Kansas City, Missouri, Hallmark has about 22,000 full-time employees and 12,000 part-time employees. Together Hallmark and Ambassador share the world's largest creative staff— 700 artists, designers, writers and editors who generate more than 18,000 greeting card designs annually. In addition to cards, Hallmark produces 6,000 related products, including gift wrap, calendars, mugs and party goods. To create all these designs, Hallmark counts on a large pool of freelance talent, to supplement their in-house creative staff.

Hallmark cards are carried by over 21,000 retail outlets, and Ambassador cards has an additional 16,000 accounts. Hallmark stores are independently owned, but have close ties to the home office. The only card company to advertise on television, Hallmark sponsors an entertainment series entitled "The Hallmark Hall of Fame" that is generally regarded as high caliber programming. The slogan, "When you care enough to send the very best," written in 1944, has made the name Hallmark synonymous with quality.

AMERICAN GREETINGS

American Greetings is the world's largest publicly owned manufacturer and distributor of greeting cards and personal expression merchandise. The company began in 1906 when Polish emigrant Jacob Sapirstein started a one man card-jobbing business in his adopted home of Cleveland, Ohio. Working first from a horse-drawn wagon, and later from his garage, Sapirstein's creative vision made American Greetings the industry giant it is today. The history of this company's growth is both a family and an industrial success story.

The first family member to join the firm was Jacob's nine-year-old son Irving, who became a partner in his father's business in 1918. When the entire family succumbed to a flu epidemic, young Irving ran the business alone. He called the customers, took their orders and shipped the Christmas and Valentine's Day cards that year. Irving continued to sell while creating products too. In 1960, he became president of American Greetings, and today serves as Chairman of the Board.

Brother Morris came on board in 1926, and business really started to blossom when Irving and Morris sold $24,000 worth of post cards to Euclid Beach Park in 1928. Despite the depression, the firm, then known as Sapirstein Greeting Card Company, flourished and in 1932, at Irving's suggestion, started printing their own line of cards. Jacob's youngest son Harry joined the growing firm in 1936, and in 1938 the company changed it's name to American Greetings Publishers.

Circa 1930s
Courtesy of
American Greetings Corp.

Jacob Sapirstein,
American Greetings Founder
Courtesy of
American Greetings Corp.

Mother's Day Greetings

By spreading so much gladness
You bind folks to your heart;
May you of your own sunshine
Retain a goodly part!

MADE IN U.S.A.

For Mother's Day

Greetings to Mother

Circa 1930s
Courtesy of
American Greetings Corp.

American Greetings issued its first over the counter stock in 1951, and in 1968 sales surpassed the 100 million mark. By 1982 American Greetings had become a Fortune 500 company, and today is ranked 294 on the list. Jacob Sapirstein continued to take an active part in the business until ill health forced him to retire in 1978. He died in 1987 at the age of 102.

Headquartered in Cleveland, Ohio, American Greetings has 33 plants and facilities worldwide that manufacture products printed in 16 languages. The product mix, including stationery, calendars, gift wrap, party goods and gift items, is sold through more than 90,000 retail outlets in 50 countries. Although American Greetings has a few hundred company owned stores, and products are sold through many independently owned card and gift shops, most of their distribution comes from mass retail channels such as chain drugstores and supermarkets.

American Greetings has more than 20,000 employees, including a creative staff of 500 artists, writers and designers. To complement the internal creative force, American Greetings licenses a variety of designs and characters. Some of their best known licenses include Ziggy, Holly Hobby, Strawberry Shortcake and the Care Bears.

American Greetings and their subsidiary Carlton Cards produce some 22,000 new designs each year. In 1991, sales surpassed $1.4 billion, making American Greetings, the second largest greeting card publisher in the world, with about a 30 percent share of the American market.

Circa 1940s
Courtesy of
American Greetings Corp.

Circa 1940s
Gibson Greetings, Inc.

GIBSON GREETINGS

Gibson Greetings is the oldest greeting card publisher in the United States; like Hallmark and American Greetings, Gibson began as a family operation. In 1850, the Gibson family emigrated to America. Four of the family's seven children barged a French litho press down the Miami and Erie Canal to set up shop in Cincinnati, Ohio as Gibson & Co. The four brothers made an ideal business team; Stephen, 23, always extremely artistic, gave creative direction to the earliest Gibson products. Robert, 18, with a natural talent for business management, became the office and financial advisor. George, 14, oversaw the company's press and general production, and 12-year-old Samuel assisted in all areas.

Gibson and Co. prospered as card jobbers, publishers and importers. In the early 1880's they were among the first American distributors of German fringed-edged Christmas cards, and they acted as a jobber for some of Louis Prang's earliest creations. The fifth Gibson brother, John, ran a New York based business that specialized in lithographing notes, drafts, statements, and other business oriented products. John's company merged with and separated from the Cincinnati division several times, and today operates independently as the C.R. Gibson Co. in Norwalk, Connecticut.

In 1883 Robert Gibson bought out his brother's interests, and continued to run Gibson & Co. as a sole proprietor until his death in 1895. Robert left the company to his four children: Charles R., 29; Arabella, 26; William H., 23; and Edwin P., 17, who developed The Gibson Art Company into one of America's most progressive greeting card publishers. Gibson has made many contributions to the greeting card industry, including the development of the French Fold card which permits full color printing on the cover and inside of a card to be done in one pass.

Gibson underwent two major changes in 1957; they moved into new headquarters, 10 miles north of downtown Cincinnati, and the name of the company changed to Gibson Greeting Cards, Inc. Gibson became publicly owned in 1962, and in 1964 C.I.T. Financial Corporation bought Gibson and returned it to private status. Two years after CIT's acquisition by RCA in 1980, RCA sold Gibson to former Secretary of the Treasury William E. Simon and his partner Raymond Chambers in a leveraged buyout. Simon and Chambers brought Gibson public once again, and it is currently traded on the American Stock Exchange.

Today Gibson's large staff of freelance and in-house artists and writers create several thousand designs a year. In addition to greeting cards, which account for approximately half of the company's more than $515 million in revenues, they produce party goods, calendars and giftwrap. Gibson Greetings 10 percent share of the American card market makes them the third largest greeting card publisher. Gibson's Cleo division is the largest manufacturer of giftwrap in the world.

Circa 1900s
Courtesy of
Gibson Greetings, Inc.

Circa 1940s
Courtesy of
Gibson Greetings, Inc.

At one point in time the "big three" were known as the "big five," and included two companies that are no longer in business: Norcross and Rust Craft. Like the other large firms, Norcross and Rust Craft both started out as family owned businesses and both played a major role in the greeting card industry.

RUST CRAFT

Rust Craft originated in Kansas City, Missouri in 1906, the brain child of brothers Donald and Fred Rust. Instead of staying in the midwest like their friends the Hall brothers, the Rusts moved their company to Boston in 1913 in order to be closer to paper sources. In 1955 the firm moved to Dedham, Massachusetts, where a large painting of the building was placed in the lobby. The caption under the painting read, "The house that sentiment built," which sums up both the importance of verse on a greeting card, and how Rust Craft saw itself.

In its heyday, Rust Craft was number four of the "big five" and played a major role in developing the American greeting card market. Rust Craft introduced acetate covers to the industry, and used photography extensively. Their creative staff included 100 in-house artists and a stable of more than 100 freelancers. Rust Craft, with plants in Canada, England and Monaco was one of the first companies to have worldwide distribution.

The company grew rapidly in its early years, and in the late 1950's was taken over by the Berkman Family and traded on the American Stock Exchange. Ziff Davis Publishing bought out Rust Craft and all its subsidiaries in 1977, and then spun all the companies off in 1980. C. Charles Smith of Windsor Communications bought both Norcross and Rust Craft in 1980, and in 1981 closed the Dedham plant and merged the two firms. Many of the designs that made Rust Craft and Norcross famous were sold off piecemeal in an attempt to keep the companies afloat. Unfortunately Smith could not manage to make the companies profitable again, and filed for bankruptcy in 1982.

NORCROSS

Norcross, was founded in 1914 by brother and sister team Arthur and June Norcross. Of British ancestry, the Norcross siblings were "typical New Englanders—elegant and austere." The original Norcross cards were entirely handmade and later printed in outline and colored by hand. Norcross was the first company to make printed personal greeting cards. By 1950, the company had grown to more than 1,500 employees with 120 in the art department.

The Norcrosses fostered an artistically creative environment for their staff, and enjoyed devotion and good work in return. The firm, located in New York City, hired talented artists who helped build Norcross' reputation for creativity. After the Norcrosses died in 1968, the firm was sold. A few years later, operations were moved to Westchester, Pennsylvania, but production was considerably slowed. In 1980, C. Charles Smith of Winsor Communications purchased both Norcross and Rust Craft, and merged the two companies at the Westchester location. Operations stopped in 1982 when the company filed for bankruptcy, and the greeting card industry lost two of its major players.

Out of the more than 1,000 greeting card publishers in America, most are relatively small presses that specialize in specific areas: Pop Shots is known for their wonderful three-dimensional cards; Colors by Design produces colorful calligraphic cards with heart-warming quotations; Avanti publishes appealing photographic greeting cards; Caspari offers classy, elegant cards aimed at the high-end market. Many companies have made important contributions to the development of the card industry. Art cards, one of the original "Alternative" types of greeting cards, were first imported in the late 1960's by Marcel Schurman and Gordon Fraser. Paper Moon Graphics set a trend in the 1970's by using contemporary air-brush graphics, like those popular on record jackets and greeting cards. Abbey Press, DaySpring, Jonathan and David, Leaning Tree, and Warner Press have concentrated on publishing religious/inspirational cards aimed at the growing religious marketplace. A number of large gift companies, including Applause, C.R. Gibson, Portal and Russ Berrie also do a considerable volume of card sales.

While it is impossible to discuss each and every company, there are a few "second tier" card companies that have made interesting or noteworthy contributions to the industry; Recycled Paper Products, Blue Mountain Arts and Renaissance, are relatively new companies, having started in the 1970's, Paramount and Burgoyne, began in the early 1900's.

RECYCLED PAPER PRODUCTS

Recycled Paper Products was formed as an ecology project in 1971 by college roommates Mike Keiser and Phil Friedmann. The young entrepreneurs believed that printing cards on recycled paper was technologically and economically feasible, and could help save the earth's precious natural resources. Their success was both surprising and speedy, the cards' topical humor and non-traditional artwork touched the hearts and funnybones of consumers everywhere. In twenty short years Recycled Paper Products has grown to be the fourth largest greeting card company in the world and the largest producer of alternative cards.

The cards that Recycled publishes have always been quirky, offbeat, mostly humorous and tremendously popular. Artist Sandra Boynton, well known for her wonderful animal characters and wacky, pun-filled messages, was one of the first artists to freelance for Recycled. Unlike other large card companies, Recycled does not have an in-house art staff, relying instead entirely on a group of almost one hundred freelancers. In addition to Boynton, Recycled cards feature designs by Cathy Guisewite of the "Cathy" comic strip, Nicole Hollander of the "Sylvia" strip, Barbara and Jim Dale, Kevin Pope and Kathy Davis among others.

Recycled Paper Products is a people oriented organization that has always had a relaxed work environment. In 1982, the company first instituted a dress code requiring shoes and shirts! Sales reached 50 million in the early 1980's, and in 1984 Recycled developed Recycled's Original Concept Stores—"ROCS." Independently owned and operated card and gift stores, ROCS carry 25 to 55 percent Recycled merchandise. Today there are more than 1000 ROCS nationwide.

Keiser and Friedmann still approve every one of the 3,700 new designs that Recycled produces each year. The company currently employs 410 people at their Chicago headquarters, and 700 commissioned sales people. Privately held, Recycled sells over 173 billion cards each year through their 34,000 retail outlets. This translates into sales of more than $100 million, or a 2 percent market share.

Recycled Paper Products has had a longstanding commitment to the environment and to recycling. The company has an in-house recycling program and purchases environmentally friendly supplies. Technical advances in paper production have made it possible in 1991 for Recycled to offer their entire card line on 100% recycled stock. Given the public's growing awareness of environmental problems, consumers are purchasing Recycled's cards not only because they like the designs and messages, but because they want to do something environmentally sound. Recycled hopes that this will force other card manufacturers, especially the "big three" to jump on the recycling bandwagon.

BLUE MOUNTAIN ARTS

Blue Mountain Arts was one of the first alternative greeting card companies. Started in 1971 by husband and wife team, Stephen Schutz and Susan Polis Schutz, their cards feature lengthy poems decorated with airbrush illustration. Stephen the artist, and Susan the writer, founded the Colorado based company on the principle that there was—and still is—a need for sensitive poetry printed on high quality paper. Originally they sold their cards themselves, filling orders from the back of their van. The Schutzes see themselves not as manufacturers, but as creative individuals who are filling a need.

Certainly the success of the company lends credence to their beliefs. Although Blue Mountain Arts has only four alternative card lines, they have more than 20,000 retail outlets and 100 employees. They also publish calendars, prints and books. Since their inception, Blue Mountain Arts offered specific, sensitive and supportive themes, ones which have become more and more popular. Their look, and the type of messages they offer, have not changed much in the last twenty years.

Increasing public demand for alternative cards has helped the company's growth, and also attracted attention from the "big three," who began offering alternative cards of their own. In 1986 Hallmark came out with a line called "Personal Touch" that was so similar to Blue Mountain Arts' "Airbrush Feelings" cardline that Blue Mountain Arts was able to win an injunction against Hallmark. This was a victory not just for Blue Mountain Arts, but for all small card companies, as it ensures writers and designers a measure of creative freedom.

RENAISSANCE GREETING CARDS

Renaissance began when six friends who lived in an "intentional community" in Massachusetts printed a few black and white Christmas cards in 1976. They tried to market them first by mail, then by selling the cards at craft shows and local stores, and eventually through independent sales reps throughout the country. When Renaissance came out with their first "Everyday line" in 1979, they decided to concentrate not just on the artwork, but on the sentiment as well. Trying to escape the flowery prose and rhymed verses popular on traditional cards, Renaissance wrote sentiments in "everyday language," and is known today for very meaningful, warm, personal and involving verse.

Like their Christmas cards, the "Everyday" line was well received, and in 1980 the company branched into other seasonal offerings. Renaissance relocated in 1981 to Springvale, Maine, where the business has continued to grow. The six founders each carved their own niche. Randy Kleinrock oversees all operations as Renaissance's President. Creative Director Robin Kleinrock, Randy's wife, is in charge of all product and promotion. Bill Grabin, the Executive Vice President, oversees all internal operations, and Ruth Miller, Data Processing Manager, oversees the computer system. Judy Baylies is the Sales Support Manager, and Ronnie Sellers is in charge of product development and distribution. A seventh owner, Melvin Weiner, left Renaissance in 1984 and went on to found Millrock Displays.

The original team has grown; Renaissance now has 55 employees, including a creative staff of seven. The in-house art department has worked with almost 200 freelance artists to create the charming, colorful designs for which Renaissance is known. The art department, like the rest of the company, makes all decisions by group consensus.

Because of their philosophical roots, Renaissance has evolved into a caring company whose purpose is to provide products intended to enhance relationships by supporting positive values. Despite the competitive nature of this industry, they pride themselves on dealing honorably and ethically in the marketplace, and working together to reach their goals. "The primary purpose of Renaissance Greeting Cards is to enhance the quality of life," reads the Renaissance "Mission Statement."

BURGOYNE, INC.

Burgoyne, Inc. was founded in 1907 by Sidney J. Burgoyne, an Englishman who worked as a salesman for a Philadelphia based stationer. When making his rounds, many of his customers asked him for holiday cards. The firm he worked for didn't carry Christmas cards, so he decided to fill a market void by starting a company to manufacture them.

Today Burgoyne is known in the industry as a specialist in creating top quality traditional Christmas cards. Burgoyne cards, available in boxed, counter and personalized versions, frequently utilize special treatments like foil-stamping, die-cutting or embossing to enhance their designs. Burgoyne's 3 in-house artists and 25 freelancers, help produce the 400 new Christmas card designs the company offers each year. Burgoyne also has reciprocal art agreements with companies the world over.

Unlike most firms that offer relatively equal numbers of everyday and seasonal products, Burgoyne's specialization causes a fluctuation in their work force. The 110 permanent staff swells to more than 200 employees during their busiest season, June–October. Burgoyne is a privately held, family run business; Sidney J. Burgoyne led the company until his death in 1946. A sensitive and caring man, he often spoke to his employees at Thanksgiving. One year he told them, "When we count our blessings at the holiday time, we think of friends like you."

Sidney J. Burgoyne had six sons: Sidney C., Bill, Harry, Dave, Joe and Lou, all of whom were active in the company. After their father's death, the oldest son, Sidney C., became president until his death in 1956. His brother Harry became Burgoyne's third leader until he retired in 1970 and passed the presidency on to his son James.

James started work at Burgoyne in 1962 at the age of 26, and has been extremely active in the greeting card industry. In addition to serving as both President and Chief Executive Officer of Burgoyne, he was President of the Greeting Card Association in 1991. James is proud that his three children, fourth generation Burgoynes, play a key role in the family business.

Under this leadership Burgoyne has grown considerably. Their 5000 retail outlets generated sales of more than $25 million in 1991. In an effort to further expand the business by adding strong everyday offerings, Burgoyne recently purchased California based Curtis Swann, a full service firm that specializes in embossed designs.

PARAMOUNT

Paramount was founded in 1906 by a Japanese wood and novelty company that wanted to break into the American market. A full service marketer, Paramount is known for having a traditional high quality card line. Located in Pawtucket, Rhode Island, Paramount has always been privately held. It's motto reads "cards from the heart."

In 1983, the firm was purchased by Charles Davison, who added some contemporary alternative card lines to Paramount's offerings. These alternative lines have proven to be both popular and profitable. Paramount acquired Reed Starline, a publisher of 600 designs targeting for the Christian market, in 1985. Paramount is known for specializing in ethnic cards. In addition to offering cards targeted for Jewish and Black consumers, Paramount has the largest selection of Spanish language cards in the United States.

Seasonal cards are those published for the many holidays and occasions that occur throughout the year. Seasonal cards account for roughly half of all greeting card sales in the United States. The chapters in this section contain outstanding examples of greeting cards created for the important seasonal occasions. These major occasions, and a number of minor ones are summarized on the chart below.

SEASONAL CARDS 1991
Percentage of Sales by Seasonal Card Sending Occasion

Occasion	Number of Cards Sold	Percentage of Seasonal	Percentage of Total
Christmas	2,300,000,000	58.00%	31.50%
Valentine's Day	1,000,000,000	25.00%	13.75%
Easter	155,000,000	4.00%	2.00%
Mother's Day	155,000,000	4.00%	2.00%
Father's Day	90,000,000	2.25%	1.00%
Graduation	90,000,000	2.25%	1.00%
Thanksgiving	45,000,000	1.00%	0.50%
Halloween	28,000,000	0.70%	0.35%
St. Patrick's Day	16,000,000	0.40%	0.20%
Rosh Hashanah	12,000,000	0.30%	0.15%
Hanukkah	11,000,000	0.30%	0.15%
New Year's Day	10,000,000	0.25%	0.15%
Grandparent's Day	4,000,000	0.10%	0.05%
Sweetest Day	2,000,000	0.05%	0.03%
Passover	2,000,000	0.05%	0.03%
Secretary's Day	1,600,000	0.04%	0.02%
Boss' Day	1,000,000	0.03%	0.01%
Mother-In-Law's Day	800,000	0.02%	0.01%
April Fool's Day	500,000	0.01%	0.01%
Total Seasonal	3,900,000,000	100.00%	50.00%
Total All Cards	7,800,000,000	—	100.00%

As the chart indicates, Christmas is by far the top selling occasion, with Valentine's Day second, and Easter a distant third. Together these three holidays account for more than 85 percent of all seasonal card sales.

Christmas

The actual birthday of Jesus Christ is not known, but since the year 354 the anniversary of his birth has been celebrated on December 25th. Scholars believe that this date was chosen because it coincided with the date of a Roman festival commemorating the winter solstice. The word Christmas comes from the English phrase "Christes Masse" which means Christ's Mass. In the early days Christmas was a strictly religious celebration, but as Christianity spread throughout the world church festivals added local customs. By the Middle Ages Christmas had become such a spirited event that in the late sixteenth century the Puritans outlawed the holiday!

In 1681, the law forbidding Christmas observance was repealed, and by the mid-eighteenth century the holiday was widely celebrated in both Europe and the United States. Today, it is observed the world over with a variety of interesting traditions. In the United States, the holiday is commemorated with church services, family gatherings and gift giving. In December, eighty percent of all American families decorate a Christmas tree.

Sending and receiving cards has been a cherished part of the Christmas holiday since 1843 when the first Christmas card was printed in England. This tradition began with Sir Henry Cole, the inaugurator and first director of the Victoria and Albert Museum. Upon realizing that he would be unable to personally greet everyone he wanted to at Christmas, he commissioned London artist John Calcott Horsley to paint a Christmas scene expressing his wishes for a Merry Christmas and a Happy New Year. The resulting card, sent to more than 1,000 friends and acquaintances, was so well received that by 1860 the custom of sending Christmas cards was firmly established throughout the British Empire.

In America, Christmas cards were made popular by Louis Prang, known today as the "Father of the American greeting card." Prang, a German emigrant to Boston, perfected the color lithography process, and in 1874 he began to produce Christmas cards by printing them in as many as twenty colors. The quality of his lithography, combined with the inclusion of a sentiment on the inside of the card, made Prang's publishing business quite successful. By 1880, Prang was printing more than 5 million cards a year. Cheap German imports flooded the American market in the late 1880's, and by 1890 Prang stopped publishing cards. But the public demand for Christmas cards increased, and by the early 1900's American publishers dominated the market, eliminating the need for inexpensive imports.

Today's consumers can select from thousands of different Christmas designs. Common themes include Santa Claus, holly, Christmas trees, wreaths, candy canes, winter landscapes, reindeer, doves, poinsettia and baby Jesus. More than 30 percent of all Christmas cards published today have religious designs; it is interesting to note that early Christmas cards were seldom religious in character, usually depicting flowers or children.

Christmas cards are available in boxed, personalized and counter card versions. They range from humorous to traditional in design and verse; red and green are the predominant colors. Most American families send more than 25 Christmas cards each year. In fact, about 30 percent of the 7.8 billion cards sent in America in 1991 were Christmas cards. Christmas accounts for 58 percent of seasonal card sales; this year Americans sent more than 2.3 billion Christmas cards, making Christmas 1991 the largest card sending occasion ever.

PUBLISHER
Burgoyne, Inc.
ART DIRECTOR
Bary Petit
ARTIST/ILLUSTRATOR
Michael Burd

Black is a highly unusual color for the Christmas season, but on this striking card it makes an elegant statement. Holographic foil gives the reindeer's scarf a special touch.

INSIDE SENTIMENT:

Wishing you a Beautiful Holiday Season and a New Year of Peace and Happiness.

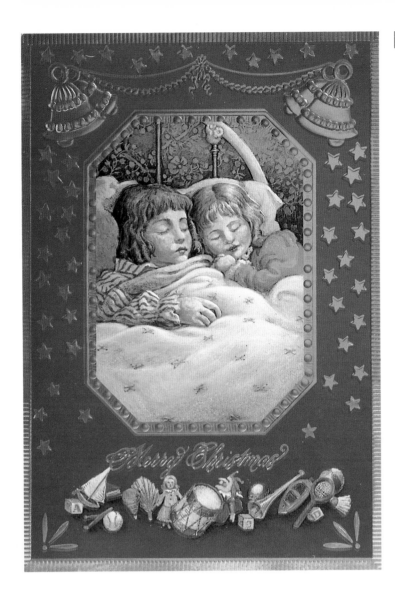

PUBLISHER
Pop Shots, Inc.
ART DIRECTOR
Paul Zalon

Pop Shots, noted for their extraordinarily fine, three-dimensional mechanical cards, created this charming illustration based on Clement Clark Moore's famous poem "A Visit From St. Nick" ("Twas the Night Before Christmas.")

PUBLISHER
Arlene Segal Designs

This striking foil-stamped appliquéd card features a rhinestone center and a beautifully calligraphed inside verse. It was nominated for a Louie Award in 1991.

INSIDE SENTIMENT:

May Christmas bring the music of laughter, the warmth of friendship & the spirit of love.

ART DIRECTOR
Paul Barchowsky
ARTIST/ILLUSTRATOR
Paul Barchowsky
CALLIGRAPHER
Nan Jay Barchowsky

A forest of Christmas trees pops up when this handmade card is opened.

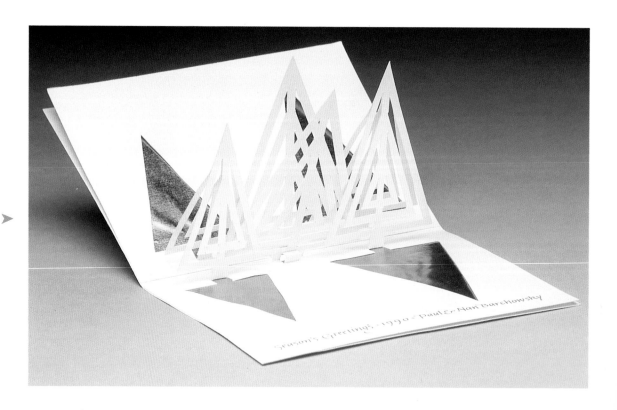

PUBLISHER
Plum Graphics Inc.

An unusual folding technique helped these three die-cut deer win a 1991 Louie Award nomination.

PUBLISHER
Meri Meri

This appliqué wreath provides the dominant design element of this Louie Award winner.

INSIDE SENTIMENT: BLANK

PUBLISHER
Linda Jade Charles

This elegant foil-stamped card with its unusual metallic star appliqué has a top fold.

INSIDE SENTIMENT: BLANK

PUBLISHER
Second Nature Ltd.

An interesting mechanical construction enables this wonderful, colorful card to spring up to stand 16 inches high.

PUBLISHER
© **Gibson Greetings, Inc.**
Reprinted with Permission
of Gibson Greetings, Inc.,
Cincinnati, Ohio 45237.
All Rights Reserved.

This charming illustra-
tion with its bright color
palette depicts nature's
joy in the holiday season.

INSIDE SENTIMENT:

*May Christmas bring you
all you're wishing
for...and more!*

PUBLISHER
Nordenhok Design, Inc.
ART DIRECTOR
**Ove Nordenhok and
Nancy Nordenhok**
ARTIST/ILLUSTRATOR
Ove Nordenhok

This elaborate die-cut design was chosen for its
unique construction and
its contemporary graphic
interpretation of Santa
Claus.

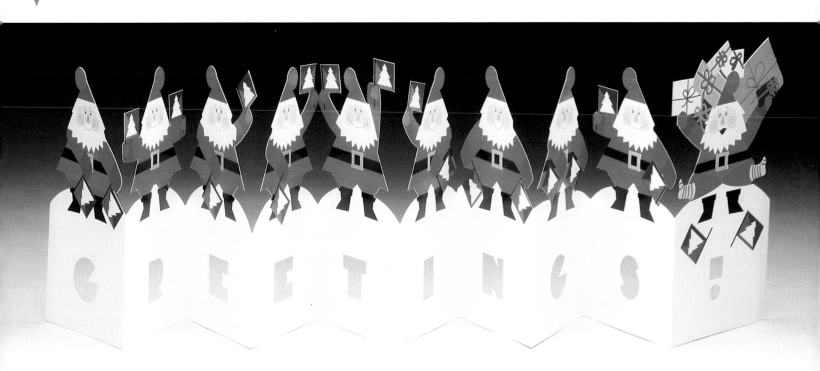

PUBLISHER
**Herlin Card, Div. of
Graphics 3 Inc.**

This nostalgic three-di-
mensional 1991 Louie
Award nominee is more
than a card—it's a
Christmas ornament as
well.

PUBLISHER
Nordenhok Design Inc.

This whimsical die-cut
1991 Louie Award winner
offers Christmas greet-
ings in many languages.

PUBLISHER
The Ampersand Studio
ARTIST/ILLUSTRATOR
Michael Laming

This nostalgic three-dimensional scene of Christmas carollers is printed front and back.

PUBLISHER
Current, Inc.
ART DIRECTOR
Merrily Johnson
ARTIST/ILLUSTRATOR
Dick Dahlquist
EDITORIAL
Nan Roloff

This unusual card has a die-cut window which allows the recipient to visualize the child's dreams. The full-color, beautifully drawn illustration printed on the inside has a sentiment that truly portrays the spirit of Christmas.

ARTIST/ILLUSTRATOR
Cathy Stork Waters

This flowing pen and ink illustration of the dove of peace was hand-painted in watercolors.

INSIDE SENTIMENT: BLANK

ARTIST/ILLUSTRATOR
Melissa Titone

High rag content paper was embossed, then hand colored and glittered to create this beautiful, contemporary Christmas card.

INSIDE SENTIMENT: BLANK

PUBLISHER
The Ampersand Studio

This card offers a twist on the traditional manger scene—a unique circular shape and a three-dimensional format.

INSIDE SENTIMENT: BLANK

PUBLISHER
Courage Center
ART DIRECTOR
Joan Hendrickson
ARTIST/ILLUSTRATOR
Carolyn Harper

This highly realistic, traditional winter landscape imparts a peaceful, serene feeling. The embossed frame border provides a subtle "fine art" appeal.

INSIDE SENTIMENT:

Wishing you a beautiful Holiday Season and a peaceful New Year.

Wishing you a World of Peace

for the Holiday Season and throughout the New Year

ORBIS TERRARUM DESCRIPTIO DUOBIS PLANIS HEMISPHÆRIIS COMPREHESA

PUBLISHER
Burgoyne, Inc.
ART DIRECTOR
Barry Petit
ARTIST/ILLUSTRATOR
Michael Burd

Fine printing techniques of embossing and die cutting on a heavy gloss-coated card stock combined with a magnificent foil appliqué make this a truly outstanding card.

33

PUBLISHER
Renaissance

This multi-fold Christmas card is die-cut to give the illustration a layered look.

PUBLISHER
Renaissance
ARTIST/ILLUSTRATOR
Kathlene Obringer

A basket of fruit rendered in unusual spring-like pastels creates a memorable card.

INSIDE SENTIMENT:

Wishing you a beautiful and bountiful holiday season filled with good friends and good cheer. Merry Christmas

PUBLISHER
Patricia Buttice
ARTIST/ILLUSTRATOR
Patricia Buttice

The deckled edge of this quality textured stock is enhanced by the understated design and elegant lettering.

INSIDE SENTIMENT: BLANK

PUBLISHER
Rohnart Inc.
ART DIRECTOR
Maria De Simone
ARTIST/ILLUSTRATOR
Victore Design Works
DESIGNER
James Victore

The musical notes on the scale are cleverly executed Christmas ornaments.

INSIDE SENTIMENT:

Wishing you a Merry Christmas and a Happy New Year

PUBLISHER
Abbey Press
ART DIRECTOR
Sharon Lueken
ARTIST/ILLUSTRATOR
Michael Kecseg

Flowing calligraphy in subtle shades of red contrasts nicely with the delicate watercolor border and illustration.

INSIDE SENTIMENT: BLANK

35

PUBLISHER
Pop Shots, Inc.

This pop-up Christmas card is beautifully illustrated and expertly engineered.

ARTIST/ILLUSTRATOR
Elyse Nierenberg

This elegant Christmas card is printed on heavy silver foil card stock. Individually die-cut white paper doves are hand tied onto the card via silver cord.

INSIDE SENTIMENT: BLANK

PUBLISHER
Gordon Fraser, Inc.
ART DIRECTOR
Andrew Brownsword
ARTIST/ILLUSTRATOR
Kathryn White

An elegant wraparound poinsettia design is beautifully printed on the gold background of this extraordinary card.

INSIDE SENTIMENT:

Peace and happiness for Christmas and always

Valentine's Day

There are many different stories about the origin of celebrating February 14 as Valentine's Day, and it is difficult to know which of the interesting legends associated with the holiday have a factual basis. One of the most popular stories is told of a Christian martyr, Valentinus, who was jailed in 270 by Emperor Claudius II for refusing to renounce his Christianity. While in jail he befriended the jailer's blind daughter and restored her eyesight. Before his February 14th execution, Valentinus left a parting note for the girl signed with the now famous words, "from your Valentine."

In Terni, Italy, the leader of the region's Christian community was named Valentino. Before he was beheaded on February 14, 270, he kept a garden where lovers could meet. Another story is told of a Roman priest named Valentine who played cupid to couples barred from marriage by Claudius II. Before he was discovered and imprisoned, Valentine secretly married couples. He died in jail on February 14, 269. February 14 was also the date of the Roman feast of Lupercalia—a celebration in which young men would draw names of maidens who they would then court throughout the year. Whatever its origin, Valentine's Day has become a day for lovers everywhere.

Valentine's Day was the first holiday when people exchanged written greetings. The first known card was a love note smuggled from the Tower of London in 1445. By 1667 it was common for men proposing marriage to handwrite and decorate Valentine's Day messages. Handmade cards continued to be popular until the early nineteenth century, when the first ready-to-send Valentines were published. In the 1840's Esther Howland became the first commercial Valentine publisher in America.

The years between 1840 and 1860 are considered the golden age of Valentines. It was a time when paper laces of extreme delicacy, expert design and workmanship were being made. Hand painted illustrations of cupids, flowers, hearts and birds—the same motifs still used to decorate cards today—were pasted on top of the lace. As late as 1939 cards were still being hand colored, and even in the early 1950's real lace was often used. Red has always been the premiere color of the day, although pink, white, gold and lavender are frequently seen.

In addition to sending a Valentine, February 14th is usually celebrated with romantic dinners and by sending flowers, chocolates or other tokens of affection. Although usually thought of as a romantic holiday for lovers, Valentines today are also sent to friends and teachers; three out of four Valentines are sent to relatives. Men buy more Valentines than any other kind of card with those addressed to "wife" and "sweetheart" being the two top selling captions. Most Valentine's Day cards are traditional, romantic and sentimental, but humorous Valentines are gaining steadily in popularity. About 25 percent of the more than one billion Valentine's Day cards Americans exchanged in 1991 were sent by children.

PUBLISHER
Linda Jade Charles Design

The doors on this wonderfully creative Valentine open to reveal a hand-lettered message.

PUBLISHER
**Linda Jade Charles
Designs**

A stunning baroque heart is foil-stamped on the cover of this Valentine. The silver and red lace bow adds a striking touch.

INSIDE SENTIMENT: BLANK

PUBLISHER
Curtis Swann
ARTIST/ILLUSTRATOR
Jane Dunworth

This intricately embossed and red foil-stamped Louie Award Winner features a typographic design.

FOR MY
WONDERFUL WIFE
ON VALENTINE'S DAY

PUBLISHER
© **Gibson Greetings, Inc.,**
Reprinted with Permission
of Gibson Greetings, Inc.,
Cincinnati, Ohio 45237. All
Rights Reserved.

Red is the color most
often associated with Valentine's Day. This Victo-
rian fan is unique due to
its non-traditional color
palette and scalloped
edge.

INSIDE SENTIMENT:

With All My Love
I love the closeness that
we know, the things we're
always sharing…, I love
our times together filled
with tenderness and
caring…

I love the many ways you
show I mean so much to
you…
and that you love me,
too.
HAPPY VALENTINE'S
DAY

PUBLISHER
Cardtricks
ART DIRECTOR
Simms Taback

Multiple colors and an intricate die cut make this Louie Award nominee spring into motion.

INSIDE SENTIMENT: BLANK

PUBLISHER
Raecath, Inc.
ART DIRECTOR
Kinka Zimmie
ARTIST/ILLUSTRATOR
Kinka Zimmie

The traditional Valentine's Day heart theme is softly rendered in colored pencil.

INSIDE SENTIMENT:

I'm bringing you all the love I could gather up in my heart.
Happy Valentine's Day

PUBLISHER
Michel & Company
ART DIRECTOR
Michel Bernstein
ARTIST/ILLUSTRATOR
Angela Zannetides Sinno

The unique die-cut and unusual fold of this card allows the sender to pen their own heartfelt message.

PUBLISHER
Pop Shots, Inc.

A gift tag is attached to this elegant three-dimensional card of a single rose.

PUBLISHER
Michel & Company

Reproductions of antique Victorian ephemera decorate this special die-cut card.

Easter

Easter, one of the holiest Christian holidays, commemorates the resurrection of Jesus Christ and the promise of eternal life. The holiday was named after Eostre, the Anglo-Saxon goddess of spring. In the United States, Easter is celebrated on the first Sunday following the first full moon after the vernal equinox, the beginning of spring. The actual date varies from year to year, falling anywhere from March 22nd to April 25th.

The first Easter card dates back to around 1908. Today, Easter is the third largest card sending holiday, surpassed only by Christmas and Valentine's Day. In 1991 Americans sent more than 155 million Easter cards, 70 percent of which went to relatives. Easter has a large percentage of juvenile card senders and receivers, and the Easter bunny, which has great appeal to children, is frequently used. Another traditional design motif is the egg, which is considered a symbol for new life and resurrection. Decorating Easter eggs is an art form that dates back to the Middle Ages. In European countries ornately decorated eggs are often exchanged as gifts.

Other themes that are frequently illustrated on Easter cards include flowers, particularly lilies and tulips, and Easter baskets. Shades of green, purple, white and yellow, colors associated with spring, are most widely used. Green, nature's most abundant color, symbolizes new life; royal purple represents mourning; pure white symbolizes light and joy; and yellow signifies radiance. Design styles range from traditional religious to the humorous, with the majority of Easter cards being sweet, and with cute illustrations.

PUBLISHER
Gordon Fraser, Inc.
ART DIRECTOR
Andrew Brownsword
ARTIST/ILLUSTRATOR
Kate Veale

Sweet illustrations, hand lettering and muted colors are the components of this oversized Gordon Fraser card.

Hoping that your Easter ... is full of ... delightful surprises!

PUBLISHER
The Ampersand Studio
ARTIST/ILLUSTRATOR
Roy Laming

This lovely three-dimensional floral basket bears an Easter greeting.

PUBLISHER
Colors by Design
ART DIRECTOR
Tamara Harrell
ARTIST/ILLUSTRATOR
Stephen Davis

Bold, bright colors make this watercolor of an Easter basket appealing.

INSIDE SENTIMENT:

Wishing you all the joys of Spring

PUBLISHER
Michel & Company
ART DIRECTOR
Michel Bernstein
ARTIST/ILLUSTRATOR
Michel Bernstein

A scalloped, die-cut edge and stylized illustration provide a finishing touch for this appealing Easter card.

INSIDE SENTIMENT:

Oh, the happiness of Easter

FOR YOU,
Mom
and Dad
WITH A WORLD
OF LOVE

PUBLISHER
© **American Greetings Corporation**

This egg-shaped card is enhanced with a pearlized foil treatment.

INSIDE SENTIMENT:

Family ties are precious bonds that passing time endears. They're ties that seem to deepen and grow stronger through the years...

Family ties are joyful bonds that bring us special pleasure through happy times and memories we'll always treasure. Family ties are lasting bonds woven in each heart that keep the family close in thought—together or apart!

Fondest thoughts of all the things that both of you have done. Warm memories of the times we've shared, the laughter and the fun. All these come with wishes and more love than words can say to fill this Easter message for the two of you today.

Have a Wonderful Easter

Mother's Day

The tradition of honoring mothers with their own special day was established in England in the mid-nineteenth century. In 1872 Julia Ward Howe, author of "The Battle Hymn of the Republic," first suggested that Americans also observe a mother's day. But the founding of Mother's Day in this country is credited to Anna Jarvis, a Philadelphia spinster who on the second anniversary of her mother's death, May 9, 1907, began a letter writing and speaking campaign to promote the national observance of Mother's Day.

Her efforts proved successful when on May 8th, 1914 President Woodrow Wilson officially declared that the second Sunday in May would henceforth be known as "Mother's Day." Jarvis started the tradition of wearing a colored carnation to honor a mother who is living, and a white carnation to honor a mother who has died. Since then greeting cards have become an integral part of the celebration.

Mother's Day is a sentimental holiday, and traditional feminine designs of flowers and hearts are two of the best selling motifs. Soft spring colors, reds, pinks and mauves most frequently grace the covers of Mother's Day cards.

Changing family relationships have made an impact on this holiday and expanded the need for cards. Non-traditional titles including "step-mother" and "like-a-mother" are the fastest growing in the category. This year over 30 million Mother's Day cards were purchased for someone other than the sender's own mother. In 1991 Americans sent nearly 155 million Mother's Day cards making it the fourth largest seasonal card sending occasion.

PUBLISHER
Curtis Swann
ARTIST/ILLUSTRATOR
Nancy Clairmont

An embossed, open die-cut design forms the cover of this Mother's Day card.

INSIDE SENTIMENT: BLANK

PUBLISHER
Old Print Factory

The circular image on this unusual Louie Award nominee was taken from a turn of the century antique paper collection.

PUBLISHER
Avanti
ART DIRECTOR
Michael Quackenbush
PHOTOGRAPHER
Dennis Mosner

This adorable photograph says, "Happy Mother's Day."

INSIDE SENTIMENT:

At your service!
Happy Mother's Day

PUBLISHER
© Gibson Greetings, Inc.
Reprinted with Permission of Gibson Greetings, Inc., Cincinnati, Ohio 45237. All Rights Reserved.

A graphic illustration in southwestern colors adorns this embossed, oversized card.

INSIDE SENTIMENT:

If I had to say why I love you, I wouldn't know where to start—
For I love you for everything you are, And I love you with all my heart!
Happy Mother's Day

PUBLISHER
Michel & Company

This lovely die-cut card offers an unusual design of an envelope containing a note card.

PUBLISHER
Colors by Design
ART DIRECTOR
Tamara Harrell
ARTIST/ILLUSTRATOR
Stephen Davis

A bright, watercolor floral border decorates this Mother's Day card.

INSIDE SENTIMENT: BLANK

Father's Day

In 1910 Louisa Dodd, the daughter of a Civil War veteran, started a movement to establish a day to recognize fathers. Fourteen years later, President Calvin Coolidge wrote the nation's governors asking them to observe a Father's Day in their respective states. Although observance of the holiday quickly became widespread, it was not until 1974 that President Nixon signed a congressional resolution legally establishing a Father's Day as a national holiday to be celebrated on the second Sunday in June.

Popular Father's Day motifs include outdoor and sports scenes, boats, cars, trains and wildlife. Colors have traditionally been masculine—blues, browns, greens and gold, but have become more vibrant in recent years. Although classic sentimental designs always sell well, many Father's Day cards are written in a humorous vein. Father's Day is the fifth largest card selling holiday. In 1991 more than 90 million Father's Day cards were sold.

PUBLISHER
© **Gibson Greetings Inc.**
Reprinted with Permission of Gibson Greetings, Inc., Cincinnati, Ohio 45237. All Rights Reserved.

This soft, colored-pencil drawing of a classic car theme conveys warm Father's Day wishes.

INSIDE SENTIMENT:

It's fun to go for rides with you And play our games together too— We're real good buddies, you and me, And you're the best dad there can be!
HAPPY FATHER'S DAY!

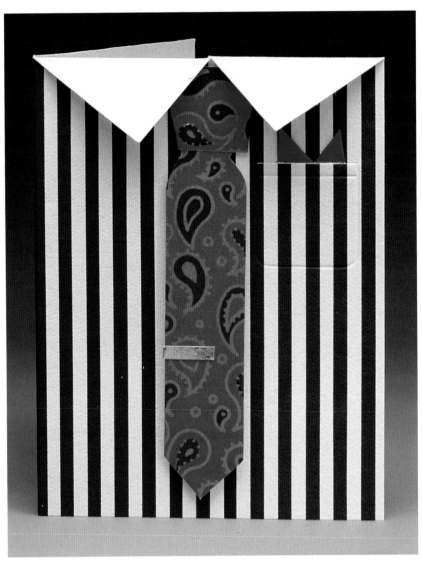

PUBLISHER
Meri Meri
ART DIRECTOR
Meredithe D'Arcy
ARTIST/ILLUSTRATOR
Kathryn Cross
EDITORIAL
Meredithe D'Arcy
DESIGN CONSULTANT
Keiko Otsulca

This bold appliqué and die-cut card showcases masculine attire.

INSIDE SENTIMENT: BLANK

PUBLISHER
Ambassador Cards
ART DIRECTOR
Betty Harlin-Roy
ARTIST/ILLUSTRATOR
Paula Hayek
EDITORIAL
Kay Andrew

This tri-fold Father's Day card contains exuberant illustrations and multi-colored, glittery stars.

PUBLISHER
Meri Meri
ART DIRECTOR
Meredithe D'Arcy
ARTIST/ILLUSTRATOR
Leslie Cesarz
EDITORIAL
Meredithe D'Arcy
PRINTER
Moquin Press

This Louie Award nominee has a charming appliquéd teddy bear to express the holiday's theme.

INSIDE SENTIMENT: BLANK

PUBLISHER
© **American Greetings Corporation**

This graphic landscape silhouette has great masculine appeal.

INSIDE SENTIMENT:

Although we think of those we love, We sometimes fail to show it—Guess it's just because we feel that somehow they should know it—But, Dad, in case you're wondering, This comes to make it clear—You're thought of in the warmest way every day, all year! Happy Father's Day

ON FATHER'S DAY

PUBLISHER
© **Gibson Greetings Inc.**
Reprinted with Permission of Gibson Greetings, Inc., Cincinnati, Ohio 45237. All Rights Reserved.

Bright colors and a nautical theme combine nicely with the blue background on this Father's Day card. Another nautical illustration is printed inside in four-color.

INSIDE SENTIMENT:

For the love you show, for the things you do, and just being you... HAPPY FATHER'S DAY WITH LOVE

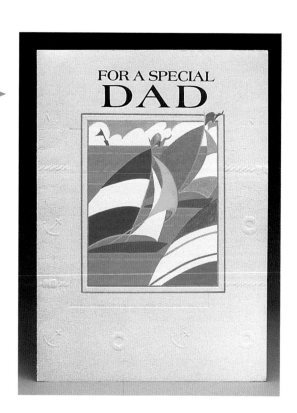

FOR A SPECIAL DAD

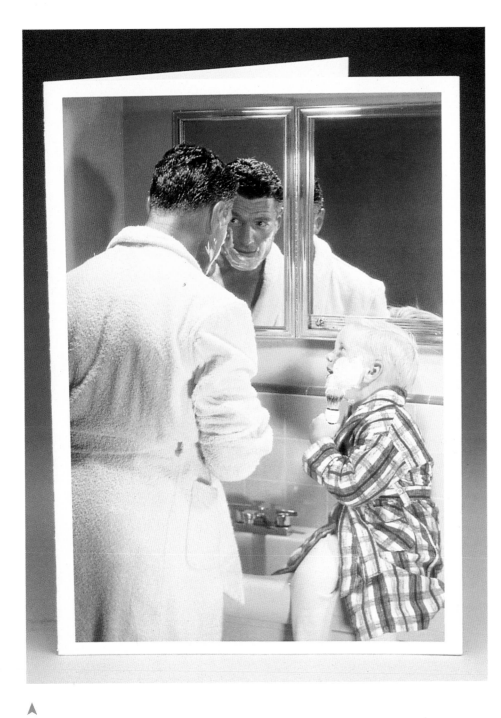

▲

PUBLISHER
FPG International
PHOTOGRAPHER
**FPG International/
L. Willinger**

The nostalgic photograph of a father and son shaving works well with the sentiment, "We've been through a lot of close shaves together." This card was a Louie Award nominee.

PUBLISHER
Hallmark Cards, Inc.

This die-cut card is folded twice to give the impression of layers. The handkerchief pulls out of the sportscoat pocket.

INSIDE SENTIMENT: BLANK

Graduation

Cards to congratulate the graduate have been around since the turn of the century. Early graduation cards were often decorated with paintings of imagined rosy futures, golden clouds and fairylike scenes of splendor. The messages tended to be on the serious side including words of advice and good wishes.

Contemporary graduation cards frequently have cute illustrations and humorous verses. Some of the traditional design elements include diplomas, mortarboards, stars, rainbows and flowers. Like any congratulatory occasion, balloons, streamers and confetti painted in bright cheerful colors are also used. Graduation is the sixth largest seasonal card-sending occasion. In 1991, graduates received more than 90 million cards.

PUBLISHER
**Recycled Paper
Products, Inc.**
ARTIST/ILLUSTRATOR
McDonald
EDITORIAL
McDonald

A cartoon graphic in combination with a humorous sentiment creates a special card.

INSIDE SENTIMENT:

THANK GOD!

PUBLISHER
Colors by Design
ART DIRECTOR
Tamara Harrell
ARTIST/ILLUSTRATOR
Stephen Davis
EDITORIAL
Peggy Dugan-French

Bright colors and contemporary graphics decorate this festive card.

INSIDE SENTIMENT:

You made it with flying colors!
Congratulations on your Graduation

PUBLISHER
Oatmeal Studios

This humorous, unusually colored card is designed to be sent from a parent to a child.

INSIDE SENTIMENT:

love,
Mom and Dad

PUBLISHER
Avanti
ART DIRECTOR
Michael Quackenbush
PHOTOGRAPHER
Dennis Kitchen

This upbeat photograph enhances the sentiment printed on the card's interior.

INSIDE SENTIMENT:

You Made It!
Congratulations

PUBLISHER
Marian Heath Greeting Cards, Inc.
ARTIST/ILLUSTRATOR
Joanne Fink, Janet Hoffberg

The watercolor rainbow painting provides a soft backdrop for the hand-lettered caption on this graduation card.

INSIDE SENTIMENT:

Let the brightness of your dreams guide the way to a happy and successful future!

PUBLISHER
Renaissance
ARTIST/ILLUSTRATOR
Rita Marandino

This serious card with a beautiful rose border offers inspiration to the graduate.

INSIDE SENTIMENT:

Wishing you a world of happiness and the fulfillment of your dreams. Congratulations!

Halloween

The Halloween holiday, once known as Samhain, was originated by the Celtic Druids as a fall harvest feast close to 2,000 years ago. The Druids believed that on October 31st, the end of summer and the beginning of their new year, witches, ghosts and other spirits roamed. In medieval times October 31st also marked All Hallows Eve, a religious observance to honor the dead. The Druid observances influenced and then merged with the Christian festival, and gradually the holiday now known as "Halloween" emerged.

Through the centuries Halloween lost its religious significance but maintained its association with ghosts and other spirits. Modern Halloween traditions include carving pumpkins into jack-o-lanterns, costume parties, bobbing for apples, and every child's favorite—dressing up for trick-or-treat.

Although widespread American observance of Halloween began in the mid-nineteenth century, it was not until 1908 that the first Halloween greeting cards appeared, and not until the past two decades that they really became popular. Orange and black, the classic Halloween colors, lend themselves to strong graphic designs. Card images include almost anything scary, haunted houses, bats, black cats, monsters and skeletons, not to mention ghosts, witches and other spirits. Friendlier Halloween motifs include pumpkins and candy corn. Many Halloween cards are written in a lighthearted or humorous vein. Children, who especially enjoy this holiday's customs, receive half of the more than 28 million cards exchanged at Halloween.

PUBLISHER
Del Rey Graphics

An appliqué of a witch flying on her broomstick gives this wonderful Louie Award winner a three-dimensional appeal.

INSIDE SENTIMENT:

Happy Halloween

PUBLISHER
**Marcel Schurman
Company, Inc.**
PHOTOGRAPHER
Katrine Naleid

The winsome photograph gives this card broad consumer appeal.

INSIDE SENTIMENT:

*Happy Halloween,
Pumpkin*

PUBLISHER
Great Arrow Graphics
ART DIRECTOR
**Alan Friedman, Donna
Massimo**
ARTIST/ILLUSTRATOR
Lisa Sarach

A silk screen of a bevy of bats silhouetted against a full moon provides a contemporary Halloween graphic.

INSIDE SENTIMENT:

Happy Halloween

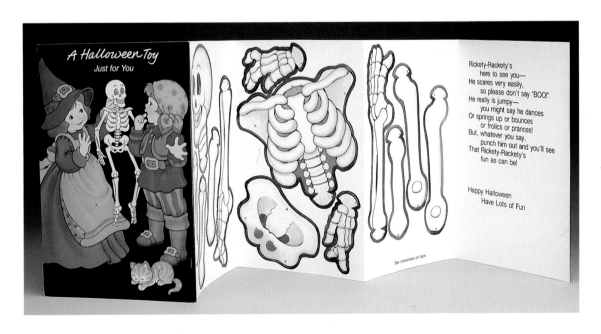

PUBLISHER
**© American Greetings
Corporation**

This juvenile Halloween card contains a skeleton paper doll which can be punched out and put together.

PUBLISHER
Paramount Cards Inc.
ART DIRECTOR
Linda King
SVP CREATIVE & EDITORIAL
Richard Kreider

A cartoon portrait of a witch with glitter application gives the illustration a tactile feel.

INSIDE SENTIMENT:

Witching you a Happy Halloween!

PUBLISHER
Widget Factory Cards
ART DIRECTOR
Suzy Becker
ARTIST/ILLUSTRATOR
Suzy Becker
EDITORIAL
Suzy Becker

A simple, humorous illustration is the main focus of this Louie Award nominee.

INSIDE SENTIMENT:

Celebrate Mischief!

PUBLISHER
Hallmark Cards, Inc.

An intricate, laser-cut, folded graveyard adds a mysterious touch to this haunting Halloween card.

PUBLISHER
Hallmark Cards, Inc.

This special card has an unusual die cut and fold, and it also glows in the dark!

Good E-e-e-evening!

PUBLISHER
Rohnart Inc.
ART DIRECTOR
Maria De Simone
ARTIST/ILLUSTRATOR
David Martin

This simple silver ghost was foil stamped on duplex paper. The graphic, hand-lettered interior message adds to the dynamic design.

INSIDE SENTIMENT:

Boo!

Hanukkah

In 165 B.C.E. the king of Syria tried to abolish the Jewish faith by killing the Jews or forcing them to convert. A small band of patriots led by Judah Macabee fought and miraculously defeated the large Syrian army and ended the fierce religious persecution. Upon reclaiming their desecrated temple from the Syrians, the Jews found enough oil to keep the sacred temple lamp lit for only one day. By some miracle, the oil lasted eight days, during which time the temple was rebuilt.

The Hebrew word Hanukkah means dedication, and this festival of lights commemorates the rededication of the temple in Jerusalem. Hanukkah is celebrated for eight days, beginning on the 25th day of the Hebrew month of Kislev, which usually falls sometime in December.

Hanukkah is a family holiday with many interesting traditions; exchanging cards is a common custom. Blue, white and gold are considered Hanukkah colors, and most cards feature one or more of the traditional Hanukkah motifs, dreidels or spinning tops, six pointed stars of David and families lighting the Menorah, a nine branched candelabrum. In 1991, 11 million Hanukkah cards were purchased.

PUBLISHER
Hallmark Cards, Inc.

This gorgeous hand-lettered card features beautifully designed Hebrew calligraphy, gold printing and striking colors.

INSIDE SENTIMENT:

May this holiday season hold many special joys for you.

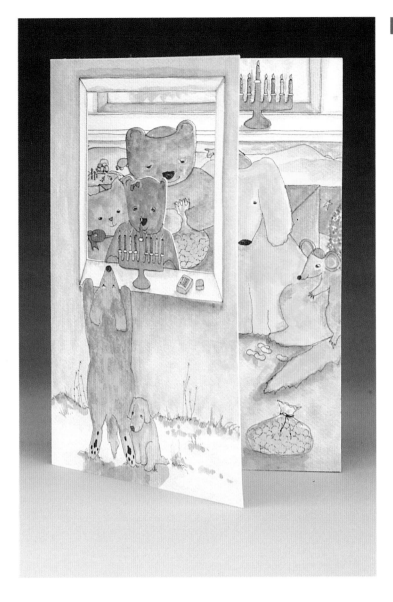

PUBLISHER
Pinx A Card Co., Inc.
ART DIRECTOR
Ricky Goodman
ARTIST/ILLUSTRATOR
Cecie McCaffery
EDITORIAL
Cecie McCaffery

This card is printed four-color on both sides. The die-cut embellishes the charming family illustration.

DREIDEL, DREIDEL, DREIDEL
I MADE IT OUT OF CLAY, AN
D WHEN IT'S DRY AND REA
DY, THEN DREIDEL I SH
ALL PLAY ✡ DREIDEL, DR
EIDEL, DREIDEL, I MADE IT
OUT OF CLAY, AND WHEN IT
S DRY AND READY, THEN D
REIDEL I SHALL PLAY ✡
DREIDEL, DREIDEL, DREIDEL, I MADE IT OUT OF CLAY, AND WHEN
IT'S DRY AND READY, THEN DREIDEL I SHALL PLAY ✡ DREIDEL,
DREIDEL, DREIDEL, I MADE IT OUT OF CLAY, AND WHEN IT'S

HAPPY HANUKKAH

DRY AND READY, THEN DREIDEL I SHALL PLAY ✡ DREIDEL,
DREIDEL, DREIDEL, I MADE IT OUT OF CLAY, AND WHEN IT'S D
RY AND READY, THEN DREIDEL I SHALL PLAY ✡ DREIDEL, DREIDE
L, DREIDEL; I MADE IT OUT OF CLAY, AND WHEN IT'S DRY AND READ
Y, THEN DREIDEL I SHALL PLAY ✡ DREIDEL . DREIDEL, DREIDEL, IM
ADE IT OUT OF CLAY, AND WHEN IT'S DRY AND READY, THEN DREID
EL I SHALL PLAY ✡ DREIDEL, DREIDEL, DREIDEL, I MADE IT OUT O
F CLAY, AND WHEN IT'S DRY AND READY, THEN DREIDEL I SHALL
PLAY ✡ DREIDEL, DREIDEL, DREIDEL, I MADE IT OUT OF CL
AY, AND WHEN IT'S DRY AND READY, THEN DREIDEL I SH
ALL PLAY ✡ DREIDEL, DREIDEL, DREIDEL, I MADE IT OUT OF
CLAY, AND WHEN IT'S DRY AND READY, THEN DREIDEL I
SHALL PLAY ✡ DREIDEL, DREIDEL, DREIDEL, I MADE IT OUT OF
CLAY, AND WHEN IT'S DRY AND READY, THEN DREIDEL I SHALL
PLAY ✡ DREIDEL, DREIDEL, DREIDEL, I MADE IT OUT OF CLAY, AN
D WHEN IT'S DRY AND READY, THEN DREIDEL I SHALL PLAY
✡ DREIDEL, DREIDEL, DREIDEL, I MADE IT OUT OF CLAY, AND
WHEN IT'S DRY AND READY, THEN DREIDEL I SHALL PL
AY ✡ DREIDEL, DREIDEL, DREIDEL, I MADE IT OUT O
F CLAY, AND WHEN IT'S DRY AND READY, THEN DREIDEL
I SHALL PLAY ✡ DREIDEL, DREIDEL, DREIDEL, I MADE IT OUT
OF CLAY, AND WHEN IT'S DRY AND READY, THEN DREI
DEL I SHALL PLAY ✡ DREIDEL , DREIDEL, DREIDEL, I
MADE IT OUT OF CLAY, AND WHEN IT'S DRY AND
READY, THEN DREIDEL I SHALL PLAY ✡ DREIDE
L, DREIDEL, DREIDEL, I MADE IT OUT OF
CLAY, AND WHEN IT'S DRY AND RE
ADY, THEN DREIDEL I SHALL
PLAY ✡ DREIDEL, DREIDEL, ™
REIDEL, I MADE IT OUT
OF CLAY, AND WHE
N IT'S DRY AN
D REA
DY

PUBLISHER
All Star Paper Company
ART DIRECTOR
Sheila Stieglitz
ARTIST/ILLUSTRATOR
Jennifer Friedman

The graphic for this card, the classic dreidel, is created entirely out of letters. Bright colors add charm and appeal.

INSIDE SENTIMENT:

Wishing You Bright & Happy Holidays

PUBLISHER
Sharon Scheirer; Crockett Collection
ARTIST/ILLUSTRATOR
Dale Jackson

This Star of David, an important Jewish symbol, was produced with a silk-screen technique in primary colors.

INSIDE SENTIMENT:

May the Bright Lights of Hanukkah Shine for you throughout the Year

PUBLISHER
Clearwater Graphics, Inc.
ART DIRECTOR
Sandy Gullikson
ARTIST/ILLUSTRATOR
Sandy Gullikson
EDITORIAL
Sandy Gullikson

This extraordinary card showcases classic Hanukkah motifs associated with the holiday.

INSIDE SENTIMENT:

Happy Hanukkah!

PUBLISHER
Recycled Paper Products, Inc.
ARTIST/ILLUSTRATOR
Susan Allen

This sweet, homey scene is an unusual Hanukkah illustration because the menorah is not the focal point of the design.

INSIDE SENTIMENT:

Wishing You A Warm And Wonderful Hanukkah

PUBLISHER
**Carole Smith Gallery
Inc.**
ARTIST/ILLUSTRATOR
Jean Arnold

A stylized menorah, shaded in earth tones, is a dominant design element on this card.

INSIDE SENTIMENT:

Happy Hanukkah

PUBLISHER
Great Arrow Graphics
ART DIRECTOR
**Alan Friedman,
Donna Massimo**
ARTIST/ILLUSTRATOR
Alan Friedman
PHOTOGRAPHER
Donna Massimo

This graphic, hand silk-screened dreidel design was a 1990 Louie Award winner.

INSIDE SENTIMENT:

Happy Chanukah

WISHING YOU... THE JOY OF HANUKKAH EACH AND EVERY NIGHT!

PUBLISHER
All Star Paper Company
ART DIRECTOR
Sheila Stieglitz
ARTIST/ILLUSTRATOR
Sivia Katz
EDITORIAL
Roberta Shevin

This tri-fold Louie Award nominee features a mosaic menorah.

An Everyday card is one that can be sent on any day of the year. The "everyday category" is divided into two parts; occasion and non-occasion. An occasion is an event, like a birthday or engagement, that prompts someone to send a card. Everyday cards revolve around life-cycle events, such as a birth or a marriage. Every day is somebody's birthday or anniversary.

A non-occasion card usually falls under the headings of friendship, encouragement or romantic love. Non-occasion cards are most often sent for no particular reason other than to let the recipient know they are being thought about.

Birthday is the largest seller in the "everyday" card category; approximately 60 percent of "everyday" card sales come from Birthday cards. Anniversary is a distant second, with 10 percent of everyday card sales. Friendship, which includes other non-occasion cards, follows at 9 percent; Get Well and Sympathy, 6 percent each; Wedding, 4 percent; Baby Congratulations and Thank You each account for around 3 percent. Everyday cards, more than their Seasonal counterparts, really help people stay in touch with one another.

Anniversary

Wedding anniversaries are happy occasions in a married couple's life that are frequently celebrated with romantic candlelight dinners, flowers and gifts from one spouse to the other. Friends and relatives who wish to commemorate the special day frequently do so by sending an anniversary card.

Anniversary cards were first published in England, and have been available in the United States since the early 1900's. They are often decorated with hearts, flowers, champagne glasses, and two figures (people, teddy bears or other animals) embracing. All colors are used on general Anniversary cards. Special cards are designed for milestone 25th "silver" and 50th "golden" anniversaries.

Anniversary cards account for 10 percent of "everyday" card sales, and almost 5 percent of total card sales. In 1991 Americans sent more than 200 million anniversary cards. The theme of this occasion—love—is reflected in both the card's design and verse. Men buy 14 percent of all Anniversary cards.

PUBLISHER
Renaissance
ARTIST/ILLUSTRATOR
**Joanne Fink,
Janet Hoffberg**

This embossed, foil-stamped tri-fold, created using layers of handmade paper, was nominated for a Louie Award in 1990.

PUBLISHER
Allport Editions
ART DIRECTOR
Gordon Chun Design
ARTIST/ILLUSTRATOR
Donna McGinnis
EDITORIAL
Ardys Allport

This charming illustration, rendered in prismacolor and graphite, shows an unusual motif for an anniversary card.

INSIDE SENTIMENT:

Happy Anniversary

PUBLISHER
Englehart
ARTIST/ILLUSTRATOR
Terry Englehart

The abstract musical design clearly reflects the timeless Shakespearean quote.

INSIDE SENTIMENT: BLANK

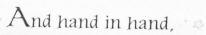

PUBLISHER
**© American Greetings
Corporation**

Two teddy bears dancing in the moonlight create a romantic mood that is carried out with the lovely sentiment.

INSIDE SENTIMENT:

Of all the places in the world, I like being with you the best!

PUBLISHER
Bottman Design, Inc.
ART DIRECTOR
Paris Bottman
ARTIST/ILLUSTRATOR
Paris Bottman
EDITORIAL
Paris Bottman

This pair of bears dancing the tango is tenderly illustrated. This card was nominated for a Louie Award in 1990.

INSIDE SENTIMENT:

Love is like dancing. When you find the right partner, it's easy!

Baby

The birth of a child is surely one of the most meaningful events in any parent's life. The new baby is welcomed by friends and relatives with gifts, cards, and good wishes. Pink is the traditional color for girls, blue for boys, and yellow is used when the sender doesn't know the child's gender. Most baby congratulations cards have sweet illustrations painted in soft pastels. Cards usually have drawings of cute infant related items—cribs, cradles, bottles, stuffed animals, rocking horses and other toys. A stork carrying a newborn is another commonly used theme.

Sales of baby congratulations cards have recently increased, due to the baby boom generation's reaching childbearing years. In 1990 more than four million babies were born in America, which resulted in the sale of over 60 million baby congratulations cards.

PUBLISHER
Paper House Productions
PHOTOGRAPHER
Jeffrey Milstein

This photographic die-cut card is blank inside.

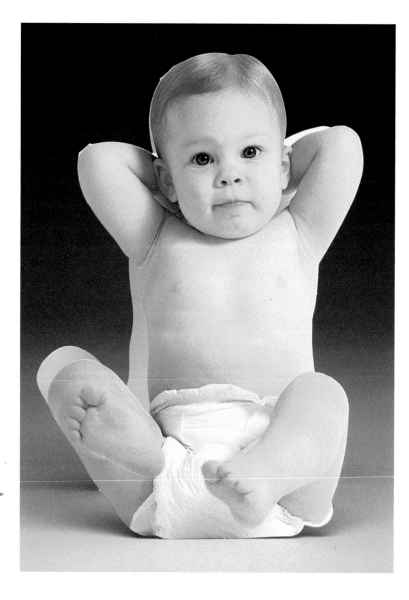

PUBLISHER
Old Print Factory

The three pieces of this nostalgic 1991 Louie Award nominee are attached with ribbons.

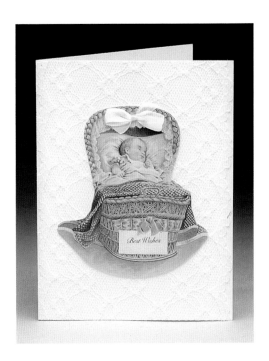

▲

PUBLISHER
Sincerely Yours
ART DIRECTOR
Genevieve Kowalchuk

The baby in the cradle appliqué was reproduced in the U.S.A. from a personal turn-of-the-century antique paper collection owned by Ralph and Diane Hellebuyck.

INSIDE SENTIMENT: BLANK

PUBLISHER
© **American Greetings Corporation**

The French fold format provides for a full color outside and inside to this card. The message, drawn out of children's blocks, and the touch of glitter on the moon and stars, add to its appeal.

INSIDE SENTIMENT:

May every star that shines in the night shine for your child—with love, warmth, and happiness!
Congratulations

PUBLISHER
Gina Bugée Karl
ARTIST
Gina Bugée Karl

This sweet card was nominated for a Louie Award in 1990.

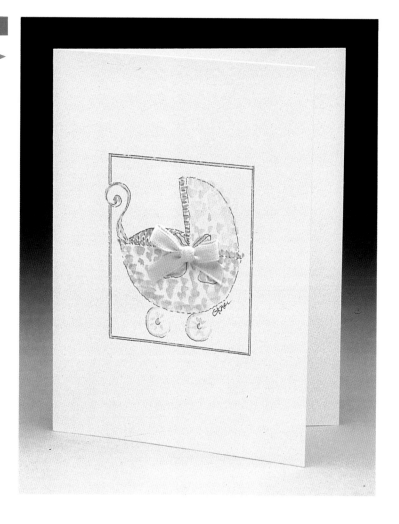

PUBLISHER
Michel & Company
ART DIRECTOR
Michel Bernstein
ARTIST/ILLUSTRATOR
Michel Bernstein

This sweetly drawn card shows the recurring moon theme which is frequently used on Baby Congratulations cards.

INSIDE SENTIMENT:

They say babies are made in heaven

▲

PUBLISHER
Paramount Cards Inc.
ART DIRECTOR
Linda King
SVP CREATIVE & EDITORIAL
Richard Kreider

This finely detailed painting, executed in soft watercolors, is a wonderful welcome for a new baby.

INSIDE SENTIMENT:

With warm congratulations on your brand-new baby boy, This greeting brings warm wishes for a lifetime full of joy... And as you watch him learn and grow, you'll come to realize The happiness he's given you will last for all your lives.

PUBLISHER
Palm Press
PHOTOGRAPHER
Michael Cardacino

The art work for this whimsical card is a photograph entitled "Special Delivery."

INSIDE SENTIMENT:

Congratulations On Your Special Delivery!

▶

Birthday

Birthday cards first appeared in England in the mid 1850's around the same time that Christmas cards became popular, and were soon being published in America as well. Many Christmas cards of this era had general illustrations of flowers and children, which could be easily adapted for birthdays simply by changing the title and sentiment. In the early 1900's, as the public's demand for cards specifically designed and written for birthdays increased, publishers began to offer a greater selection.

Birthdays in the United States are frequently celebrated with family get-togethers where a birthday cake is served and cards and presents given to the person who is turning a year older. Many children and some adults have parties to commemorate their special day. Everybody, no matter what their socio-economic, religious, or age group has a birthday. Card companies publish a multitude of birthday cards designed to appeal to the wide variety of needs and tastes expressed by the American public.

Birthdays are happy occasions, and many cards are designed with festive motifs like balloons, streamers, party hats, cake, candles and confetti. Floral designs are always popular for women, as are landscapes and sports scenes for men. Something about growing older lends itself to humor, and humorous birthday cards account for almost 30 percent of those sold. Next to Christmas, more birthday cards are sent each year than any other kind of card; they account for 60 percent of everyday card sales. Fifty-eight percent of the more than 2 billion birthday cards purchased in 1991 were received by women.

PUBLISHER
Second Nature, Ltd.

This three-dimensional birthday card explodes into a cake and party trimmings when opened.

PUBLISHER
© **American Greetings
Corporation**

This joyous, oversized card has an unusual vertical opening. Touches of glitter, and a hand lettered message make it a festive card.

PUBLISHER

C.R. Gibson—Creative Papers

ARTIST/ILLUSTRATOR

Dena

This delicate illustration is nicely set off by a scalloped edge. The box on the cover is die-cut, and opens to reveal a bouquet of flowers inside.

INSIDE SENTIMENT:

To You

PUBLISHER

Recycled Paper Products

Well known greeting card designer Sandra Boynton created this three pan-elled birthday card using a Southwestern theme.

PUBLISHER

© Gibson Greetings, Inc.
Reprinted with Permission of Gibson Greetings, Inc., Cincinnati, Ohio 45237. All Rights Reserved.

The hand-lettered message and gold foil stamping complement the abstract floral design.

PUBLISHER

© American Greetings Corporation

A romantic, ethereal feeling is created by die cutting around the edges of the clouds in this soft watercolor design. Heavily textured paper, a foil stamped message and a tipped in inner blue sheet add to its appeal.

INSIDE SENTIMENT:

I wish you a day that touches your heart, a day that's warm with the love we share, a day to cherish like the way I cherish you.
Happy Birthday With My Love

PUBLISHER
Portal Publications, Ltd.

This adorable photograph is a perfect way to wish a cat lover a happy birthday.

INSIDE SENTIMENT:

Celebrate...It's Your Birthday

PUBLISHER
Marcel Schurman Company, Inc.

The beautiful pictorial lettering of this oversized multi-fold card appeals to children of all ages.

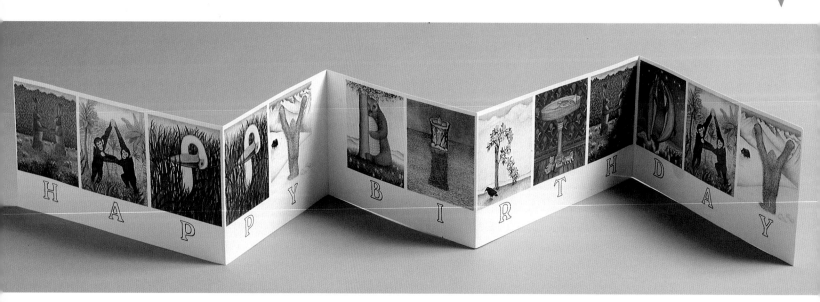

PUBLISHER
AMCAL
ARTIST/ILLUSTRATOR
Kim Jacobs

A charming illustration captures this cat's mischievous personality.

INSIDE SENTIMENT:

I've been a little wrapped up...Sorry I missed your Birthday

PUBLISHER
Carole Smith Gallery Inc.
ARTIST/ILLUSTRATOR
Marie Powell © 1991

This illustration would appeal to male card buyers and recipients.

INSIDE SENTIMENT:

Happy Birthday

PUBLISHER
Gordon Fraser, Inc.
ART DIRECTOR
Andrew Brownsword
ARTIST/ILLUSTRATOR
Kate Veale

The "doors" on this unusual oversized birthday card open to reveal a whimsical illustration.

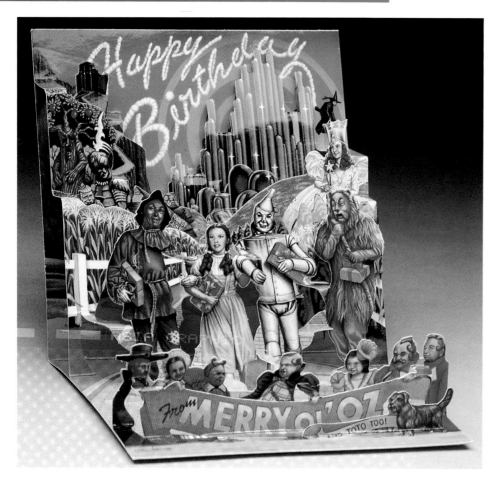

PUBLISHER
Pop Shots, Inc.

A scene from the "Wizard of Oz" comes alive when it pops out of this three-dimensional card.

PUBLISHER
Second Nature, Ltd.

Holographic foil adds color and dimension to this adorable card.

INSIDE SENTIMENT:

Have a great day!

PUBLISHER
Fravessi

The message in this die-cut 1991 Louie Award nominee is printed in both English and French.

INSIDE SENTIMENT:

Allons! Le jour de gloire est arrive! Here's to many more glorious Birthdays!

PUBLISHER
© **American Greetings Corporation**

The wonderful illustration on this multi panelled card practically sings "Happy Birthday."

Blank

One of the many reasons that greeting cards are so popular in America has been the decline of social correspondence. Now people send a card instead of taking the time to write a letter. There are still individuals who like to combine the beauty and artistry of a greeting card with a hand written note. Blank cards meet this need perfectly.

The wide assortment of strikingly designed blank cards enables the consumer to select one that will visually enhance their message, and set an appropriate tone. A blank card can be used either for a specific holiday or no occasion at all. Fine art paintings, florals, landscapes and wildlife photographs are frequently used as cover designs. Blank cards range in design from elegant to whimsical; most do not have any words. They have been increasing in popularity in the last decade.

PUBLISHER
Hallmark Cards, Inc.
ART DIRECTOR
Bill Tinker
ARTIST/ILLUSTRATOR
Ted Jordon

This striking, colorful card is embossed and has a coordinating yellow sheet tipped inside.

PUBLISHER
Portal Publications, Ltd.
ART DIRECTOR
Tina Higgins
ARTIST/ILLUSTRATOR
Tracy Reid

The interplay between color and design make this a unique floral card.

PUBLISHER
Evergreen Press, Inc.
ARTIST/ILLUSTRATOR
From an original oil painting by Laura Regan

Clean, rich colors make the dynamic oil painting, "McCaws," a contemporary masterpiece.

PUBLISHER
Cardtricks
ART DIRECTOR
Simms Taback
ARTIST/ILLUSTRATOR
Reynold Ruffins

This creative greeting card is printed front and back to simulate two sides of a playing card.

PUBLISHER
Great Arrow Graphics

The oriental flavor of this striking hand silk-screened card helped it win a Louie Award nomination.

PUBLISHER
Art Cards, Inc.

A dramatic swash of color combined with varying graphic illustrations and musical notations makes a strong statement on this artistic card.

◄ PUBLISHER
Hallmark Cards, Inc.

This unique die-cut card shows both front and back views of a charming doll.

PUBLISHER
© **Carlton Cards**

Matte black serves as a backdrop to bring out the softness of the pink calla lilies.

PUBLISHER
Carolyn Bean

A beautifully photographed winter landscape provides perfect material for this Sierra Club Christmas card.

PUBLISHER
AMCAL

The extraordinary photo-realistic quality of this landscape painting pictures nature at its best.

PUBLISHER
Red Farm Studio
ART DIRECTOR
Carmen Howard, Lisa Harter Saunders
ARTIST/ILLUSTRATOR
Linda Blackburn

"Hats on a Rack" has a feminine, old world appeal.

PUBLISHER
Allport Editions
ART DIRECTOR
Gordon Chun Design
ARTIST/ILLUSTRATOR
Robin Eschner

The highly stylized farm scene is rendered in unusual tones.

PUBLISHER
Carole Smith Gallery Inc.

This magnificent card was chosen for the quality and detail of the watercolor painting, "Awakening."

PUBLISHER
Van Dexter Cards

Florals frequently decorate blank cards, as this beautifully illustrated one exemplifies.

PUBLISHER
Blue Sky Publishing
ARTIST/ILLUSTRATOR
Sherrie Lovler

Although it is unusual to include words on the cover of a blank card, this calligraphic quote and watercolor illustration combine beautifully.

Why not go out on a limb? That's where the fruit is.
— WILL ROGERS

PUBLISHER
Curtis Swann
ARTIST/ILLUSTRATOR
Rita Marandino

The lovely rose pattern on this card is brought out by the deep embossing.

PUBLISHER
C.R. Gibson—Creative Papers
ARTIST/ILLUSTRATOR
Kurt Van Dexter

This card contains a pastel colored floral design that prints continuously on the front and back. The interior is tipped in on a separate sheet of paper.

PUBLISHER
**Marcel Schurman
Company, Inc.**

Gold foil and blind embossing add a striking touch to this brightly colored card.

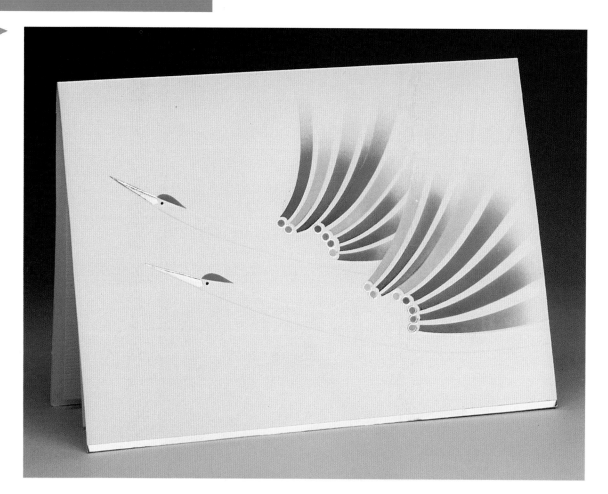

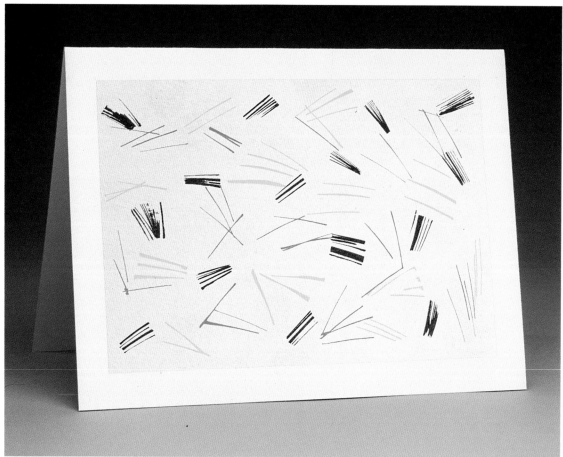

PUBLISHER
Great Arrow Graphics

A rich metallic gold background enhances the cover of this hand silk-screened card.

PUBLISHER
**Marcel Schurman
Company, Inc.**

This oriental design was printed in Japan on gold foil and tipped onto an elegantly patterned background. The separate writing sheet glued inside has an all over watermarked fan design.

PUBLISHER
**Marcel Schurman
Company, Inc.**

This handsome card was hand silk-screened in Japan on textured paper. The design carries onto the back of the card.

Congratulations

General congratulations cards acknowledge the achievements and/or good luck of the recipient. They can be sent for a variety of situations: a new job, a promotion, winning an award or even the lottery! They are always festive and upbeat, and are usually painted in bright, vivid colors. The lettering is frequently the strongest design element with bold cartoon letters or contemporary brush scripts that can be enhanced with balloons, streamers and confetti. Characters in a celebratory mood are also used to decorate cheerful congratulations cards.

PUBLISHER
Allport Editions
ART DIRECTOR
Sue Kapsos
ARTIST/ILLUSTRATOR
Linda Bacon
EDITORIAL
Michael Allport

A beautifully rendered, fine illustration of a champagne bucket and bouquet of roses makes an elegant and sophisticated card design.

INSIDE SENTIMENT:

Congratulations

PUBLISHER
Second Nature

This explosive pop-up card from the United Kingdom is a perfect way to send a congratulatory message.

Encouragement

Encouragement cards are designed to offer support to people who are going through a difficult period in their lives, such as job loss, a long term illness or the break-up of a marriage. Many of the illustrations are muted abstracts. The wide variety of texts available cover a multitude of possible sending situations.

The basic purpose of an encouragement card is to tell the sender, "I know things are hard for you right now, but hang in there. I believe in you and your ability to get through this." People often find it difficult to express their feelings in their own words. The vast selection of encouragement cards available makes it easy for consumers to select an appropriate message.

Relatively recent arrivals on the greeting card scene, sales of encouragement cards have been increasing dramatically since they were introduced almost twenty years ago. One of the reasons that encouragement cards are so popular is that they can be sent as a message of caring and support to anyone at any time.

PUBLISHER
Leanin' Tree Publishing Company
ART DIRECTOR
Jane Knutson
ARTIST/ILLUSTRATOR
Louise E. Grunewald
© 1988
EDITORIAL
Verse by Jan Michelsen
© 1988

Bold colors and beautiful hand lettering deliver the poignant sentiment.

INSIDE SENTIMENT: BLANK

PUBLISHER
© **American Greetings Corporation**

The mountain illustration on the front of this French-fold card beautifully complements the sentiment.

INSIDE SENTIMENT:

Believe in yourself-you can do it!

PUBLISHER
© **American Greetings Corporation**

A graphic border of stars and dots encloses the sentiment, that is nicely stamped in dark purple foil.

INSIDE SENTIMENT:

Believe in yourself. We believe in you!

PUBLISHER
© American Greetings
Corporation

The textured paper works nicely with the soft watercolor illustration on this card.

INSIDE SENTIMENT:

Just to let you know I'm with you all the way.

PUBLISHER
© **Gibson Greetings, Inc.**
Reprinted with Permission of Gibson Greetings, Inc., Cincinnati, Ohio 45237. All Rights Reserved.

This illustration visually reinforces the message found on many encouragement cards, "Hang in there."

INSIDE SENTIMENT:

Sometimes, waiting is the hardest part.

When life is
especially difficult,
the way it has been
for you lately.
it's hard to believe sometimes
that there is happiness
waiting for you
in the future,
and that there are still
reasons to hope and dream...
but there are.

PUBLISHER
Hallmark Cards, Inc.
ART DIRECTOR
Lori Stanziola
ARTIST/ILLUSTRATOR
Scott Brown
EDITORIAL
Linda Staten

Curved corners and a loose, brush stroke technique imbue this card with

INSIDE SENTIMENT:

If there's anything I can do to make your life better, please let me know…you're a very special person and your happiness matters to me.

Friendship

Cards which enable friends to send a card for no particular reason—just to stay in touch—fall under the broad heading of "non-occasion cards." "Thinking of You" and "I Miss You" are two of the most common captions in the friendship category. Recently the term "anyday cards" has been applied to the caption, because friendship cards can be sent any day of the year.

The first friendship cards appeared as early as 1900, and by 1915 they were being used to cross the miles separating good friends who cared about each other. In the early days friendship cards were simple, and usually featured a floral or nature theme. Art work on contemporary friendship cards varies from detailed illustrations of people or cute animals to colorful abstracts. Humor plays a growing role in this fast growing category. Friendship cards account for 9 percent of everyday card sales.

PUBLISHER
AMCAL

This charming illustration of two young friends was painted by Leesa Whitten.

INSIDE SENTIMENT:

Good friends, that's us!

Miss You--

miles

on

better!

on

◄ PUBLISHER
Hallmark Cards, Inc.

This watercolor illustration in soft tones continues on the back of the card.

INSIDE SENTIMENT:

Miss You—
We've got lots of smiles
and good times to catch
up on as soon as you're
better.

PUBLISHER
Applause, Inc.
ART DIRECTOR
Kathleen Corby
ARTIST/ILLUSTRATOR
Flavia Weedn
EDITORIAL
Flavia Weedn

This oversized card features a sweet illustration in Flavia's distinctive style.

INSIDE SENTIMENT:

Every gift your heart gives to others somehow comes back to you. Wishing you happiness

PUBLISHER
Applause, Inc.
ART DIRECTOR
Kathleen Corby
ARTIST/ILLUSTRATOR
Flavia Weedn
EDITORIAL
Flavia Weedn

This stunning watercolor appeals to flower lovers of all ages.

INSIDE SENTIMENT:

Some stay for awhile, leave footprints on our hearts and we are never, ever the same.

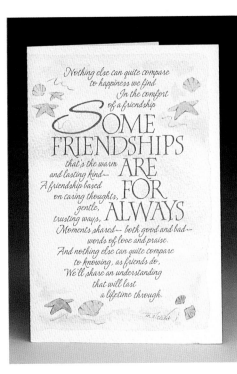

PUBLISHER
**© American Greetings
Corporation**

A textured, buff-colored paper stock adds a note of elegance to this friendship card. The main design element is the beautifully rendered hand lettering.

INSIDE SENTIMENT: BLANK

PUBLISHER
Colors by Design
ART DIRECTOR
Tamara Harrell
ARTIST/ILLUSTRATOR
Stephen Davis

This stunning watercolor appeals to flower lovers of all ages.

PUBLISHER
Carolyn Bean

Mother's Against Drunk Driving created this fun card with a serious message—"Don't drink and drive."

INSIDE SENTIMENT:

49. You and 50. Me.

PUBLISHER
© **American Greetings Corporation**

This unusually shaped card contains a continuous seascape that stretches across all three panels. Printed on recycled paper, there is an ecological message on the back of the last panel.

PUBLISHER
© **American Greeting
Card Corporation**

A hand-lettered friend-ship message stands out from a colorful rainbow wash. Shimmery glitter adds a joyful touch.

INSIDE SENTIMENT:

*Your friendship is a
bright spot in my world!*

PUBLISHER
Colors by Design
ART DIRECTOR
Tamara Harrell
ARTIST/ILLUSTRATOR
Stephen Davis
EDITORIAL
Ron Hisler

This card features a color-ful graphic and has a hu-morous inside message.

INSIDE SENTIMENT:

*How else will I know if
you have something I
might want to borrow!*

Get Well

The first get well cards were inspired by the Sunshine Society of Massachusetts in 1911 which printed small cards to send sunshine to those "shut-in" by illness. Sunshine is still frequently mentioned in the verse on get well cards today. The best selling get well designs are cheerful and bright, with encouraging images. Florals are often used along with inspirational landscapes and cute animal characters.

For those recuperating from an operation, humor usually directed at hospital food, doctors and nurses can brighten the patient's day. Sixty percent of the more than 120 million get well cards purchased in 1991 were sent to women.

PUBLISHER
Paper D'Art

This pop-up card boasts a lovely fruit basket. The hand-tied tag adds a nice touch.

PUBLISHER
The Ampersand Studio
ARTIST/ILLUSTRATOR
Roy Laming

This lovely three-dimensional card brings a bouquet of get well wishes to the recipient.

PUBLISHER
Avanti

The photograph illustrates the humorous message.

INSIDE SENTIMENT:

Get Well Soon!

PUBLISHER
Marcel Schurman Company, Inc.
ARTIST/ILLUSTRATOR
Bernard Boisson
EDITORIAL
Bonjour

The adorable photograph of a kitten snuggled up in his bed is designed to cheer up the recipient.

INSIDE SENTIMENT:

Take a few cat naps and get back on your paws real soon.

111

PUBLISHER
Renaissance
ARTIST/ILLUSTRATOR
Kathy Davis
EDITORIAL
Kathy Davis

Chicken soup is a classic home remedy for many ailments. This motif is carried out with a stylized illustration, and is printed on recycled paper.

INSIDE SENTIMENT:

Take good care of yourself and feel better soon!

PUBLISHER
Second Nature, Ltd.

This extraordinary three-dimensional get-well-soon card is manufactured in England.

This extraordinary three-dimensional get-well-soon card is manufactured in England.

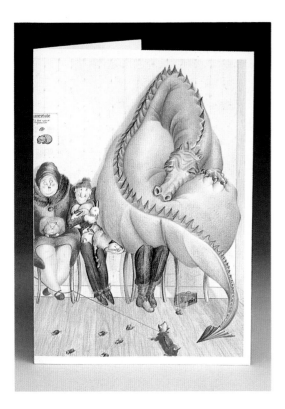

▲

PUBLISHER
Through My Eyes
PHOTOGRAPHER
Natalie Rosenthal

This humorous photograph will lighten anyone's day.

INSIDE SENTIMENT:

*I just can't bear your
being sick!
Get well soon!*

PUBLISHER
**Marcel Schurman
Company, Inc.**
ARTIST/ILLUSTRATOR
Penny Ives

A humorous, colored pencil drawing wraps around the front and back of this delightful card.

Religious

More than 60 million Americans consider themselves religious and there are different types of religious cards available to meet their needs. Most religious cards are those published with religious messages that can be sent for any everyday or seasonal occasion. Religious Christian cards are those whose verse focuses on God, Jesus and the Trinity, and are frequently scriptural in nature. The artwork on these cards usually depicts sacred symbols, or figures and events from church history. Religious/Inspirational cards have verses which pertain to love and family unity, or contain a prayer or blessing without specifically mentioning God. These cards, usually drawn in soft appealing colors, show the world in an uplifting manner.

Another type of card in this category is the Religious Occasion cards. These are designed for a religious event such as a Christening, Confirmation or Bat Mitzvah. Cards designed for Christian occasions are frequently adorned with crosses, doves, candles and church scenes. Cards designed for Jewish consumers use six pointed stars of David, Hebrew letters, Torah scrolls and other motifs particular to the occasion. Religious cards of all kinds have been growing steadily in popularity, as evidenced by the more than 70 million sold in 1991.

PUBLISHER
Renaissance
ARTIST/ILLUSTRATOR
Joanne Fink

This Passover card features a beautifully rendered illustration of a Seder plate.

INSIDE SENTIMENT:

May you and your loved ones share a holiday filled with happiness.

PUBLISHER
Caspi Cards
ART DIRECTOR
Micha Klugman-Caspi
ARTIST/ILLUSTRATOR
Micha Klugman-Caspi

This Bat Mitzvah card illustrates classic biblical characters united by a patterned border.

INSIDE SENTIMENT: BLANK

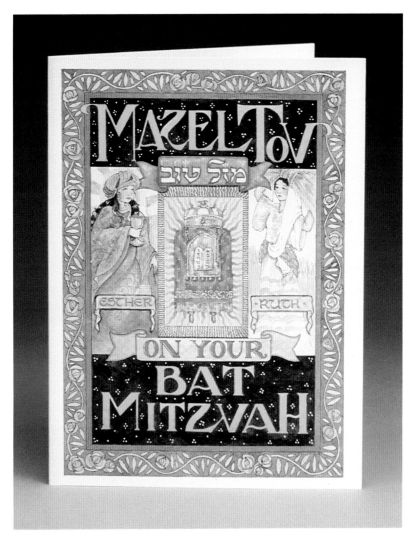

PUBLISHER
All Star Paper Company
ARTIST/ILLUSTRATOR
Janet Hoffberg

A gold foil-stamped Star of David contrasts nicely with the bright rainbow wash on the front of this Bar Mitzvah card.

INSIDE SENTIMENT:

*Today is your day.
Congratulations!*

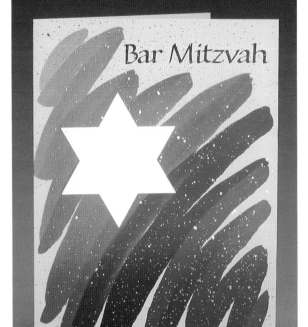

PUBLISHER
Hallmark Cards, Inc.
ART DIRECTOR
Sally Madden
ARTIST/ILLUSTRATOR
Vohnna Bandle
EDITORIAL
K. Rutz

Embossing reinforces the paper sculptured image on this monochromatic Jewish New Year's card.

INSIDE SENTIMENT:

*The High Holy Days--a time for renewing faith and hope, a time for thinking of those who are very special...a time for remembering you.
Happy New Year*

PUBLISHER
**Marian Heath Greeting
Cards Inc.**

Crosses are frequently used as religious symbols. This elegant foil-stamped silver cross is decorated with deeply embossed, pearlized flowers.

INSIDE SENTIMENT:

May thoughts of sympathy bring you comfort and may faith lighten your sorrow. With Sincere Sympathy

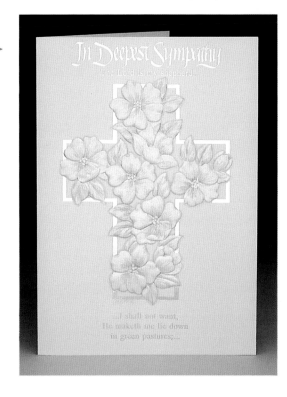

PUBLISHER
© **Gibson Greetings, Inc.**
Reprinted with Permission of Gibson Greetings, Inc., Cincinnati, Ohio 45237. All Rights Reserved.

This beautifully illustrated plastic acetate window hanging is perforated on the inside of this card so it can be removed and displayed year round.

PUBLISHER
Hallmark Cards, Inc.
EDITORIAL
Quote—R. Cusick
Sentiment—Hirschman

Soft pastels and a simple illustration effectively communicate the lovely sentiment on this card.

INSIDE SENTIMENT:

A wish that your Confirmation will only be the start of growing joy and wisdom that will fill your mind and heart.

PUBLISHER
© **American Greetings Corporation**

This tri-fold card features a keepsake Christening certificate.

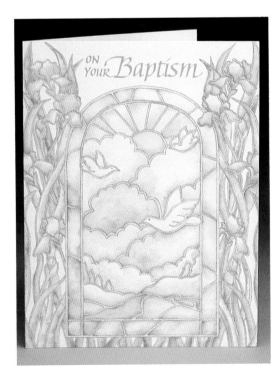

PUBLISHER
Renaissance
ARTIST/ILLUSTRATOR
Rita Marandino

A stained glass church window surrounded by irises adorns the front of this Baptism card.

INSIDE SENTIMENT:

May your life be blessed with love, peace and happiness. Best wishes on this joyful day.

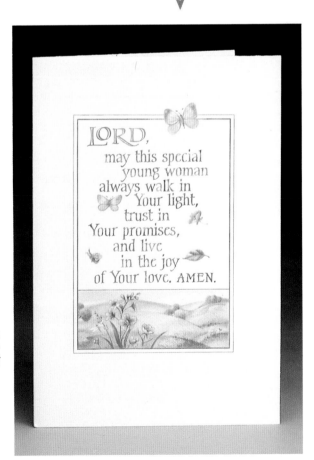

Romantic Love

Like friendship cards, romantic love cards can be sent any day of the year. There is no reason necessary other than to let that special someone know that they are loved. Whether the sender is in a relationship that is just getting off the ground, or has been married for years, the basic message of a romantic love card is to say, "I love you" to the recipient. This message can be illustrated in different ways: with a single red rose, hearts, a silhouette of a couple on a beach, or two animals in a romantic pose. The full spectrum of color is used to create a warm, romantic mood.

PUBLISHER
Ambassador Cards
ART DIRECTOR
Gail Flores
ARTIST/ILLUSTRATOR
Cathy Stafford

The warm colors of this pastel seascape work well with the romantic sentiment.

◄

PUBLISHER
Raecath, Inc.
ARTIST/ILLUSTRATOR
**From an original
painting by Kinka**

A sweet illustration of
two friends hugging
adorns the cover of this
card.

INSIDE SENTIMENT:

*Your friendship will be
remembered always.*

PUBLISHER
Recycled Paper Products
ARTIST/ILLUSTRATOR
**Laura Friedman,
David Bialek**

This pair of stylized kissing fish is rendered in an airbrush technique.

INSIDE SENTIMENT:

I think what I like best about you is how I like everything about you.

PUBLISHER
AMCAL
ARTIST/ILLUSTRATOR
Leesa Whitten

The watercolor illustration of an older couple evokes a feeling of everlasting love.

INSIDE SENTIMENT: BLANK

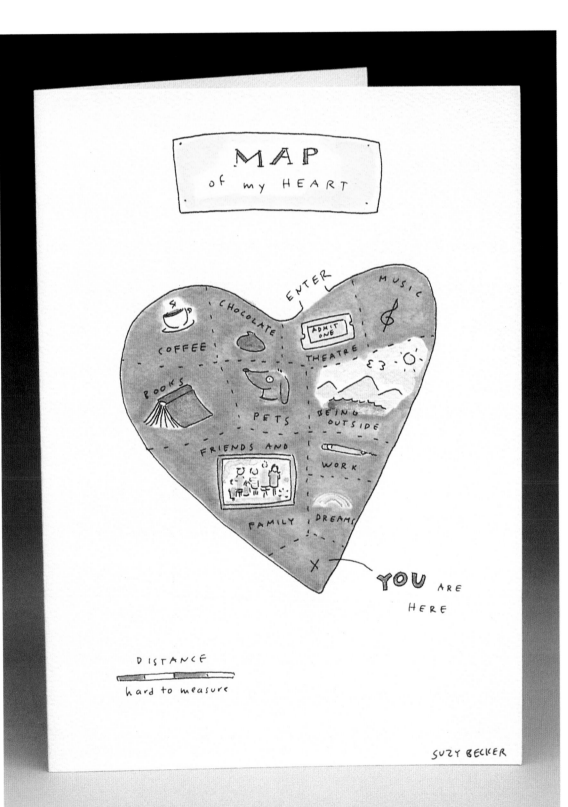

PUBLISHER
Widget Factory Cards

This lighthearted water-color evokes a warm, loving feeling.

Sympathy

It is often difficult to find the right words to say to some-one who has recently experienced a loss. Sympathy cards, which have been published since the early 1900's, let the bereaved know that they are being thought of. Designing a sympathy card is a very delicate task; the card needs to be uplifting without being upbeat and inspirational without being depressing. Above all, it needs to be comforting to the recipient.

Pastel colors, especially blues and lavenders, lend them-selves well for the muted look needed on an effective sympathy card. Irises, lilies and other flowers, soft scenic landscapes, and simple borders frequently adorned the covers of the more than 120 million sympathy cards that were sent in 1991. Forty-one percent of all sympathy cards are sent by families and 43 percent are sent to women.

PUBLISHER
Renaissance
ARTIST/ILLUSTRATOR
Kathlene Obringer

This card contains a deli-cate watercolor of lotus blossoms by Kathlene Ob-ringer and is printed on recycled paper.

INSIDE SENTIMENT:
May the love in your heart be a healing force that over time will bring you comfort and peace.

*The loss of a child
is surely the most painful hurt of all
because the love between parent and child
is the most precious love of all.*

*It is impossible to understand
why this beautiful, special person
has been taken away from us so soon.*

*There is no justice in it.
There is no reasoning to explain it.
There is no fast way to mend the hurt.*

PUBLISHER
Renaissance
ARTIST/ILLUSTRATOR
Joanne Fink
EDITORIAL
Ronnie Sellers

The subtle blending of pastels and fine lettering on handmade paper superbly delivers the tender message of sorrow for a parent whose child has died.

INSIDE SENTIMENT:

May the love in your heart be a healing force that over time will bring you comfort and peace. Our thoughts are with you during this sad time.

PUBLISHER
Idesign

The sentiment works well with the simple, serene illustration.

INSIDE SENTIMENT: BLANK

PUBLISHER
Marcel Schurman Company, Inc.
ARTIST/ILLUSTRATOR
Byung-Kap Min

Simple silver foil stamping enhances the illustration of a magnolia branch.

INSIDE SENTIMENT:

May Love Bring You Comfort And Time Bring You Peace.

▲

PUBLISHER
Carole Smith Gallery Inc.
ARTIST/ILLUSTRATOR
Joan Metcalf © 1990

This Joan Metcalf water-color, "Nunie's Garden," is a fitting and lovely complement to the printed sentiment.

INSIDE SENTIMENT:

Keep the happy memories in your heart and it will help you through this difficult time.

PUBLISHER
Marcel Schurman Company, Inc.
ARTIST/ILLUSTRATOR
Bryony Wynne Boutilier, Alexander Lavdovsky

This autumn lily was deeply embossed from hand-engraved dies.

INSIDE SENTIMENT:

In Deepest Sympathy

➤

Wedding

There are many different kinds of weddings: formal and informal, large and small, religious and secular. But all weddings are joyful occasions that give the guests a chance to share in the bride and groom's happiness. There are many interesting traditions associated with weddings. One is an old expression that encourages brides to wear "something old, something new, something borrowed, something blue." Most American brides wear a long white dress, a headpiece and veil, and carry a bouquet of flowers. They frequently borrow an old piece of jewelry, and wear a blue garter. The groom usually wears a suit or tuxedo with a boutonniere. During the wedding ceremony the couple exchange vows and rings. Afterwards there is usually a celebratory meal of some kind, complete with a tiered wedding cake with white frosting.

The earliest known wedding card dates back to 1911 and by the 1920's they enjoyed great popularity. Wedding cards almost always illustrate related items: wedding cakes, wedding bells with ribbons, a bouquet of flowers or glasses of champagne. Hearts and doves are frequently used, and some cards depict a bride and groom, or two cute characters dressed as a bride and groom, saying their vows. In 1991 more than 80 million wedding cards were purchased to wish the more than 2.4 million newlywed couples happiness.

PUBLISHER
Renaissance
ARTIST/ILLUSTRATOR
Kathlene Obringer

This tri-fold card has an unusual die-cut format and is further enhanced with embossing.

PUBLISHER
Vintage Images
ART DIRECTOR
Brian Smolens
PHOTOGRAPHER
From the Vintage Image Collection of Photographs circa 1905-1915.
EDITORIAL
Brian Smolens

A vintage photograph of two children in full wedding regalia works fantastically well with the humorous sentiment.

INSIDE SENTIMENT:

Congratulations on your marriage, kids.

PUBLISHER
Curtis Swann
ARTIST
Elyse Nierenberg

Embossing and die-cutting are two techniques utilized on this appealing 1990 Louie Award winner.

INSIDE SENTIMENT:

Congratulations on your wedding! May you have a long, happy life together.

PUBLISHER
© **Carlton Cards**

A hand-lettered sentiment adds a special touch to this lovely three-panelled card.

PUBLISHER
© **American Greetings Corporation**

A series of five die-cut hearts allows the pretty pink paper on the inside of the card to show through.

INSIDE SENTIMENT: BLANK

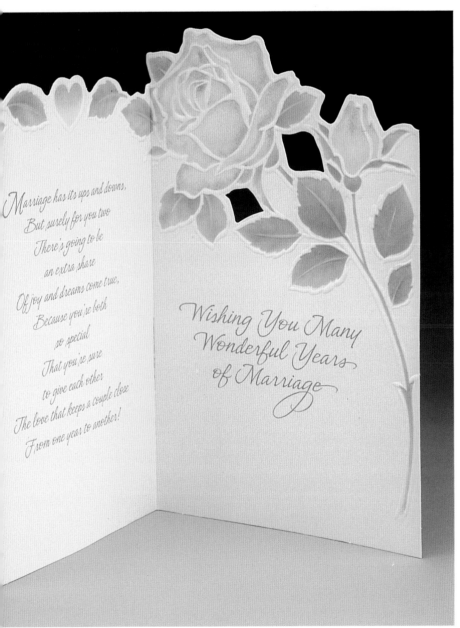

Marriage has its ups and downs,
But surely for you two
There's going to be
an extra share
Of joy and dreams come true,
Because you're both
so special
That you're sure
to give each other
The love that keeps a couple close
From one year to another!

Wishing You Many
Wonderful Years
of Marriage

All cards are special in the way they help people communicate with one another. Some cards are also considered to be special in the way they are designed or produced. This section features cards grouped together not by occasion, but by design treatment. It contains the most creative, innovative cards available in each category.

Die Cut

Modern die and laser-cut cards have their roots in the ancient art of paper cutting. Paper cutting developed in China and by the eighteenth century was widely practiced in Europe. The beautiful hand cut images were commonly used on valentines and on decorative wall hangings.

Die-cutting and laser-cutting are two different methods for creating cards with cut out images. The die-cutting process involves making a metal die that will cut the paper. This is usually done on edge or external cuts, or to create simple, usually rectangular, internal cuts. Laser-cutting involves burning the excess paper away, to leave the design behind. This technique allows for tremendous accuracy and intricate detail, such as is needed to produce a delicate lacey look. Die and laser-cut cards are often combined with embossing, or four-color process printing to create a special card that the consumer is willing to pay more for.

PUBLISHER
Hallmark Cards, Inc.

This die-cut card of a bag of French Fries is clever and fun. Glitter application on the card mimics "salt" on the French Fries.

INSIDE SENTIMENT: BLANK

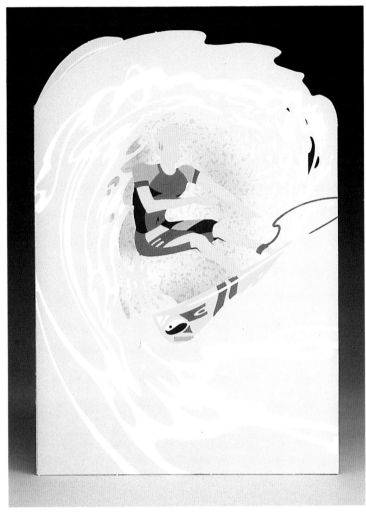

PUBLISHER
Meri Meri
ART DIRECTOR
Meredithe D'Arcy
ARTIST/ILLUSTRATOR
Michel Thomas Poulin
PRINTER
Moquin Press

Vibrant colors and die cutting are combined on this festive clown card.

INSIDE SENTIMENT: BLANK

PUBLISHER
Hallmark Cards, Inc.
ART DIRECTOR
Steve Hess
ARTIST/ILLUSTRATOR
Tom Best

This surfer card is an excellent example of an intricately laser-cut design.

INSIDE SENTIMENT: BLANK

PUBLISHER
Hallmark Cards, Inc.

This fantastic musical scale card is die cut out of duplex paper.

INSIDE SENTIMENT: BLANK

PUBLISHER
Hallmark Cards, Inc.

This tri-fold die-cut card utilizes embossing and four-color printing to add interest to the design.

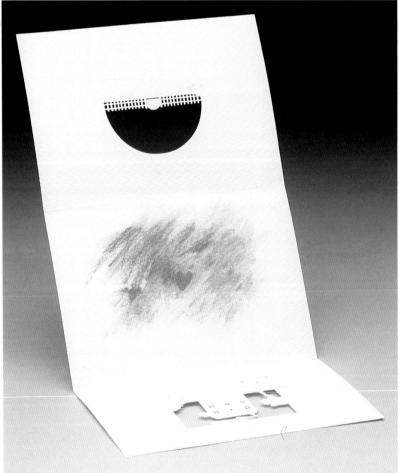

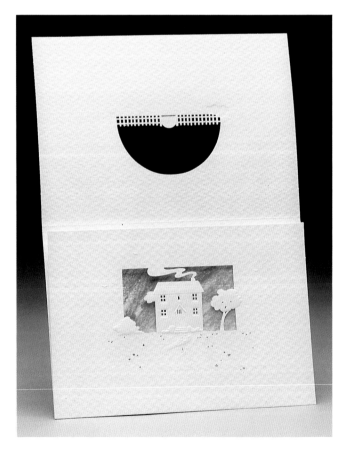

PUBLISHER
Curtis Swann
ARTIST/ILLUSTRATOR
Elyse Nierenberg

Intricate laser-cutting and deep blind embossing make this graceful scene of prancing reindeer a sophisticated card and a spectacular way to send season's greetings.

INSIDE SENTIMENT: BLANK

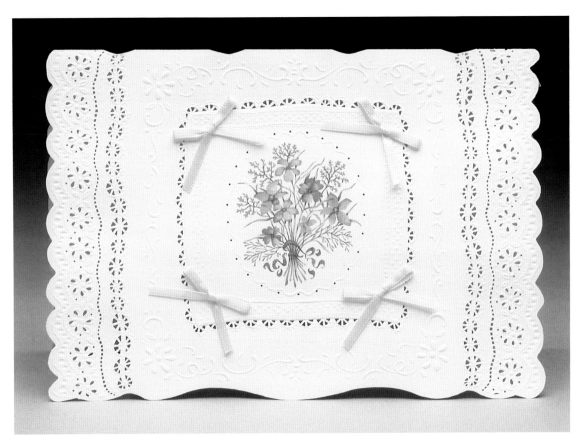

PUBLISHER
Hallmark Cards, Inc.

The delicate lacy appearance of this card is achieved through laser technology. Four pink satin bows are attached to the cover.

INSIDE SENTIMENT: BLANK

Three-Dimensional

In the late nineteenth century, elaborate, three-dimensional Valentines were first created in Germany and Belgium. It was not until 1978 that similarly complex three-dimensional "pop-up cards" were introduced in the United States. A three-dimensional card comes out of a two-dimensional format. It must be able to fold flat so the sender can write on the card and mail it.

Three-dimensional cards are more difficult, and more expensive to produce and purchase than flat cards, due to the number of tricky design and production elements involved. The concept comes first, and then the illustration has to co-ordinate with the paper engineering and die-cutting. What makes three-dimensional cards unique is that when they are opened, the inside parts spring up, and sometimes even move. Pop-up cards are extremely labor intensive, as most must be put together by hand.

To be successful as a greeting card, a three-dimensional card must have "send-ability." The piece must work as a card not just as an interesting paper construction. Most recipients keep these cards longer than flat cards, which helps three-dimensional cards enjoy a small but steady market niche.

PUBLISHER
Herlin Cards; Divison of Graphics 3 Inc.
ART DIRECTOR
Robert M. Herlin
ARTIST/ILLUSTRATOR
Cowell Hess

This three-dimensional Louie Award winning design of a piano is replete with a bouquet of roses, candelabrum and a bottle of champagne.

PUBLISHER
Courtier Fine Art Limited
ART DIRECTOR
David Pearson
ARTIST/ILLUSTRATOR
Sandy Hunt

This pop-up card is based on the children's nursery rhyme "Hey Diddle, Diddle, a Cat Played the Fiddle."

PUBLISHER
Courtier Fine Art Limited
ART DIRECTOR
David Pearson
ARTIST/ILLUSTRATOR
Sandy Hunt

When the two sides are squeezed in, this window surrounded by flowering vines turns into a three-dimensional shadow box.

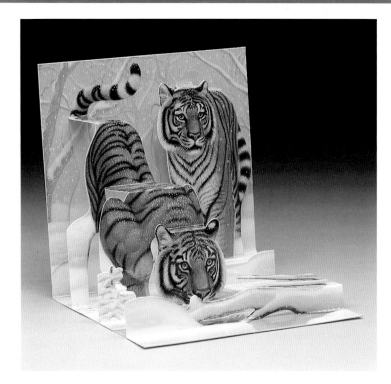

PUBLISHER
Pop Shots, Inc.

This realistically illustrated three-dimensional card is part of a series on endangered wildlife. A portion of the sales of these cards goes to the WWF (World Wildlife Fund).

PUBLISHER
Hallmark Cards, Inc.

The grass skirt of this die-cut hula dancer is attached with a brass brad. When the card is tilted, the skirt moves.

PUBLISHER
Hallmark Cards, Inc.

Two pieces of card stock glued to a red and black expandable streamer that, when pulled apart, mimics a real musical instrument. A gold and black flat braided ribbon further adds a touch of realism.

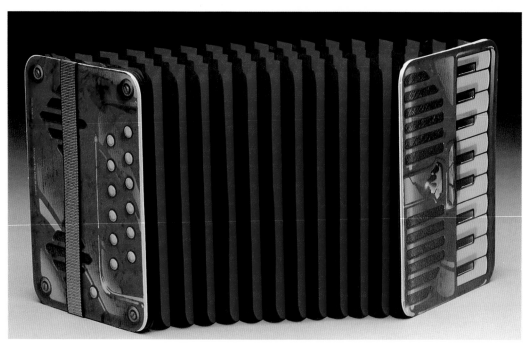

PUBLISHER
Del Rey Graphics

Metallic-red foil with glitter treatment is used in combination with unusual construction and die-cutting techniques to create this memorable card.

PUBLISHER
Herlin Cards; Division of Graphics 3 Inc.

Intricate die cuts, gluing techniques, and folds are utilized to create this outstanding three-dimensional card. The whimsical Noah's Ark design harkens to American primitive illustration.

PUBLISHER
Paper House Productions
ARTIST/ILLUSTRATOR
Jeffrey Milstein

These three house cards are die cut to form the appropriate shape. A second die cut and fold is utilized so the front doors actually open and close.

PUBLISHER
Paper D'Art

This beautifully illustrated three-dimensional card is part of the second British Bird Series. This particular card is of gold finches in a thicket of Scotch Thistle.

PUBLISHER
Herlin Cards; divison of Graphics 3 Inc.
ART DIRECTOR
Robert M. Herlin
ARTIST/ILLUSTRATOR
Cowell Hess

This Louie Award nominee becomes a carousel when removed from its envelope. A special rubber band mechanism requires no hand manipulation.

Photographic

Photography, the process that makes a picture of an object using a system of lenses and a light sensitive plate or film, was first used in 1835. The name "photography" comes from the Greek "photos" which means light and "graphein" which means to write. Black and white photographs often adorned popular nineteenth century postcards. Color photography, which developed in the late 1800's, has been used on greeting cards since the 1920's.

All greeting cards are a form of communication, and photographic cards give a literalness that is hard to achieve with other media. A recent revival of interest in photography as an art form has led to the emergence of more photographic cards in the market than have ever been seen before. The artistry of the photographer has found a perfect home on greeting cards.

PUBLISHER
Palm Press
ART DIRECTOR
Liz Bordow

This award winning humorous photograph has great appeal for all animal lovers.

INSIDE SENTIMENT: BLANK

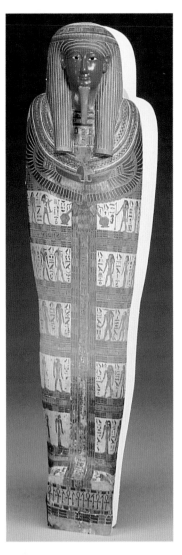

PUBLISHER
Paper House Productions
ART DIRECTOR
Jeffrey Milstein
PHOTOGRAPHER
Justin Kerr

This die-cut photograph of an Egyptian mummy sarcophagus is an unusual subject for a card.

INSIDE SENTIMENT: BLANK

PUBLISHER
Paper House Productions
ART DIRECTOR
Jeffrey Milstein
PHOTOGRAPHER
Zig Leszczynski

This unique card is die-cut in the shape of the cover photograph.

INSIDE SENTIMENT: BLANK

PUBLISHER
Avanti
ART DIRECTOR
Michael Quackenbush
PHOTOGRAPHER
Barbara Campbell

This whimsical photographic card is beautifully color-saturated. The sentiment, "I've got my eye on you!" works wonderfully with the humorous picture.

Vivid colors, glossy card stock and beautifully styled still lifes, give a painterly effect to these two special floral cards.

PUBLISHER
© **Gibson Greetings, Inc.,** Reprinted with Permission of Gibson Greetings, Inc., Cincinnati, Ohio 45237. All Rights Reserved.

INSIDE SENTIMENT:

A daughter's love warms the heart in so many beautiful ways. You're such a special daughter, it just wouldn't do to let your birthday go by without telling you how much you're loved…how much you're wished life's happiest things.
HAVE A WONDERFUL BIRTHDAY

PUBLISHER
Gibson Greetings Inc.
Reprinted with Permission of Gibson Greetings, Inc., Cincinnati, Ohio 45237. All Rights Reserved.

INSIDE SENTIMENT:

With a sister like you, how could I ever be lonely? You're always there to share a smile, listen to a problem or just talk. And whenever I need a real friend, I know I can count on you...
You're always there to make me feel special and important and loved...It's no wonder I love you so much.
HAPPY BIRTHDAY

Lettering

Text is an integral part of any greeting card and many cards feature hand-lettered captions and verses. Like illustration, lettering can be used to create a mood or feeling for the piece. Often lettering is the primary design element on a card. Letters can be written with a pen or brush, drawn and filled in, or even set in type.

Hand lettering, especially calligraphy, is often used on greeting cards. The word calligraphy comes from the Greek—"calli" which means beautiful, and "graphein" which means to write. Beautiful writing enhances a card and entices the consumer to select it. Larger card companies with in-house art staffs have entire departments devoted to hand-lettering. The artists whose work is included in this chapter have mastered the ability to make the written word both expressive and attractive.

PUBLISHER
A Hall of Gold Production
ARTIST/ILLUSTRATOR
Mike Gold

Bright colors enhance the strong graphic lettering on this card.

INSIDE SENTIMENT: BLANK

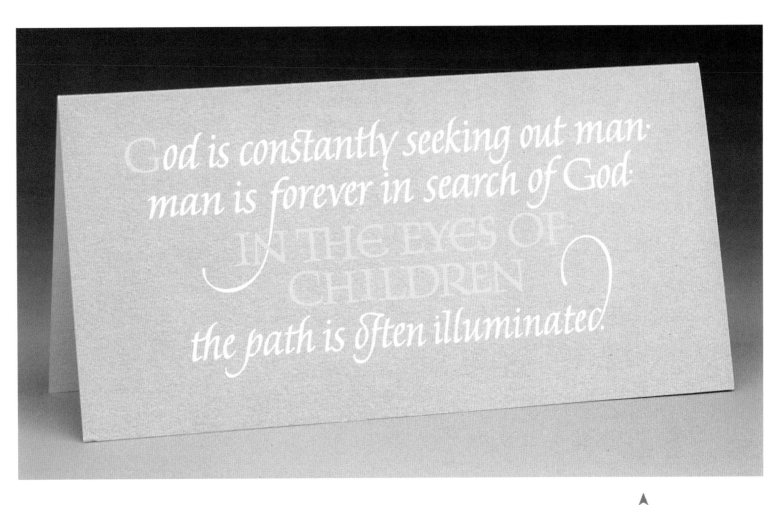

God is constantly seeking out man· man is forever in search of God· IN THE EYES OF CHILDREN the path is often illuminated·

PUBLISHER
Michael Clark
ART DIRECTOR
Michael Clark
ARTIST/ILLUSTRATOR
Michael Clark
PRINTER
Pine Tree Press

This simple two-color card was chosen for its magnificent letterforms and classic layout.

INSIDE SENTIMENT: BLANK

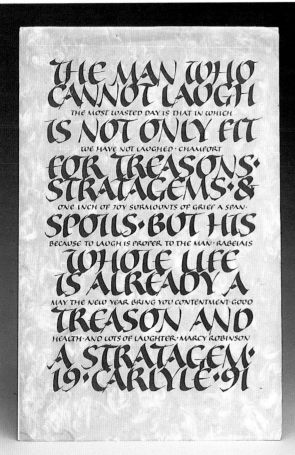

THE MAN WHO CANNOT LAUGH
THE MOST WASTED DAY IS THAT IN WHICH
IS NOT ONLY FIT
WE HAVE NOT LAUGHED · CHAMFORT
FOR TREASONS· STRATAGEMS·&
ONE INCH OF JOY SURMOUNTS OF GRIEF A SPAN·
SPOILS·BUT HIS
BECAUSE TO LAUGH IS PROPER TO THE MAN · RABELAIS
WHOLE LIFE IS ALREADY A
MAY THE NEW YEAR BRING YOU CONTENTMENT·GOOD
TREASON AND
HEALTH·AND LOTS OF LAUGHTER·MARCY ROBINSON
A STRATAGEM· 19·CARLYLE·91

ARTIST/ILLUSTRATOR
Marcy Robinson

These strong, beautifully shaped letters were screened onto delicate rice paper.

INSIDE SENTIMENT: BLANK

PUBLISHER
Anna Pinto
DESIGNER/CALLIGRAPHER
Anna Pinto

This playful Christmas card was hand colored by the artist.

INSIDE SENTIMENT: BLANK

PUBLISHER
Leanin' Tree Publishing Company
ART DIRECTOR
Jane Knutson
ARTIST/ILLUSTRATOR
Louise E. Grunewald
© 1989
EDITORIAL
Verse by Kevin Hrebik
© 1989

The colorful, circular motif creates a contrasting border for the flourished sentiment.

INSIDE SENTIMENT:

God bless you on your birthday and all through the year.

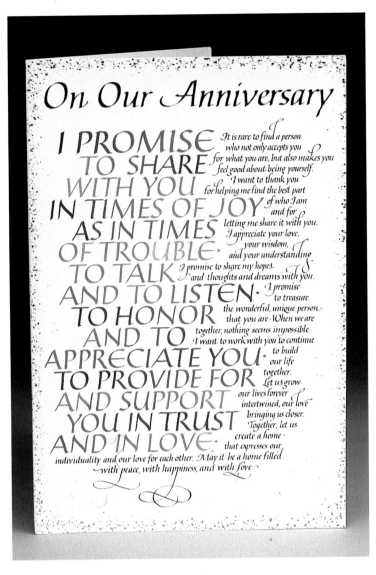

PUBLISHER
Renaissance
ARTIST/ILLUSTRATOR
Joanne Fink
EDITORIAL
Joanne Fink

Originally hand-lettered in gouache on Bristol Board, this is one of the author's favorite pieces. The gold foil stamping adds a delicate touch to the border.

INSIDE SENTIMENT:

I love you very much. Happy Anniversary!

ARTIST/ILLUSTRATOR
Pat Weisberg

This unusually constructed two-piece card was letterpress printed on a heavy textured stock. The cover design was hand colored, and complements the flourished italic lettering.

INSIDE SENTIMENT: BLANK

PUBLISHER
**Nancy Stutman
Calligraphics**
ARTIST/ILLUSTRATOR
Nancy Stutman

This colorful card was printed using a split fountain technique on heavy glossy stock.

PUBLISHER
© **American Greetings Corporation**

This trifold was selected for its subtly shaded letterforms. The contrasting sizes add interest to the design.

PUBLISHER
Gibson Greetings Inc.
Reprinted with Permission of Gibson Greetings, Inc., Cincinnati, Ohio 45237. All Rights Reserved.

This unusual vertical trifold shows lovely lettering on a layered handmade paper background.

PUBLISHER
Creative Papers by C.R. Gibson
ARTIST/ILLUSTRATOR
Timothy R. Botts

This biblical quote is a calligraphic collage of varying styles and colors.

INSIDE SENTIMENT: BLANK

Juvenile

Any card that is sent to or by a child falls into the category of juvenile cards. Juvenile cards are designed to be fun and appealing, and feature happy motifs like cute animals, clowns, cartoon characters and toys. The message is kept simple and the writing is relatively large and easy to read.

For younger children cards are often painted in soft colors, while the art work on cards designed for older children is usually executed in bright, cheerful colors. Juvenile cards are available for almost all occasions, and can include a story or game for the child to play with. Hallmark and American Greetings have recently come out with large lines targeted towards this expanding market. With more than 45 million American children under twelve, it is no wonder that 150 million Juvenile cards were sold in 1991.

PUBLISHER

Hallmark Cards, Inc.

Cartoon illustrations, bright colors and simple sentiments predominate on juvenile cards. Charles Schulz's world-famous "Snoopy" cartoon is featured on this card.

INSIDE SENTIMENT:

Awesome!

PUBLISHER
Outreach Publications
ARTIST/ILLUSTRATOR
Stephanie Stouffer

This die-cut Christmas card with its two folds plays peek-a-boo with the recipient. The sweet teddy bear makes an especially appealing card.

PUBLISHER
© **American Greetings Corporation**

This two-sided circus-clown car card features bright full-color printing on heavy coated stock.

PUBLISHER
Second Nature, Ltd.

This adorable card pops up like a real jack in the box when removed from its envelope.

PUBLISHER
Heron Arts

The image on this unique card was created entirely out of foil. The design wraps around onto the back of the card.

PUBLISHER
Creative Learning Products, Inc.
ARTIST/ILLUSTRATOR
Pat Garhart
EDITORIAL
Carol Kulina-Jegou

This creative tri-fold Louie Award nominee is designed to look like a primary school composition book. Raggedy Ann and Raggedy Andy add whimsy and color.

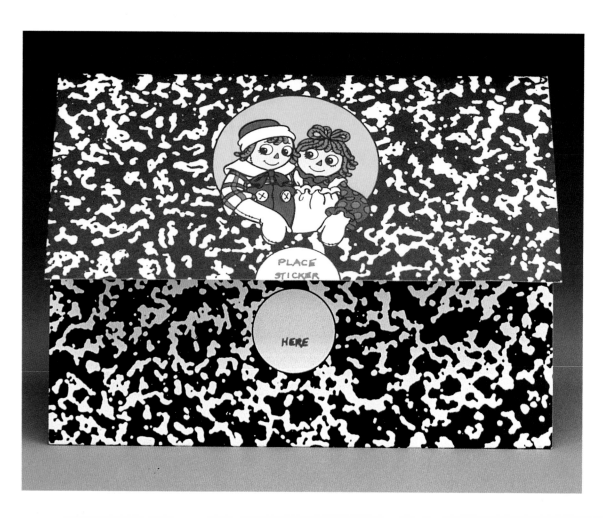

These two humorous cards were specifically created for parents to send to their children away at camp.

PUBLISHER
Contemporary Designs
ART DIRECTOR
Michael Lanning
ARTIST/ILLUSTRATOR
Debra Hamuka-Falkenham

INSIDE SENTIMENT:

Write Quick!
Lack of communication
is turning your mother
into a desperate woman.
Signed,
Joe the Postman

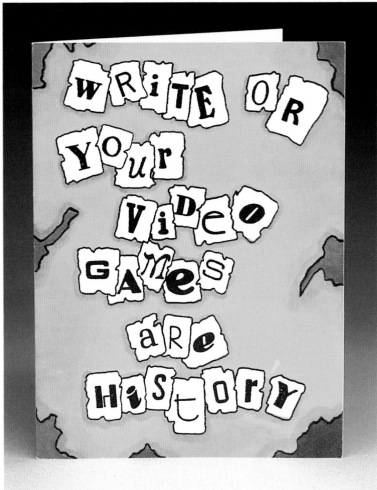

PUBLISHER
Contemporary Designs
ART DIRECTOR
Michael Lanning
ARTIST/ILLUSTRATOR
Debra Hamuka-Falkenham

INSIDE SENTIMENT:
Love, Your Mom!

Gift Cards

Some cards are more than just cards; they are a combination of a card and a small gift. "Gift cards" range from elegant to fun and usually contain some kind of keepsake such as bubble bath, a bookmark, potpourri or flower seeds that can be detached from the card for the recipient to use or keep. Although more expensive than ordinary cards, gift-cards enable the sender to communicate a sentiment and give a special gift at the same time. The high perceived value of gift-cards makes them popular items.

PUBLISHER
**Marcel Schurman
Company, Inc.**

This oriental fan card is printed on fine, gold foil paper-stock. The wood handle, affixed to the fan, further imparts an elegant air.

PUBLISHER
Hallmark Cards, Inc.

This beautifully laser-cut card contains a salmon-colored starfish stickpin for the recipient to wear.

INSIDE SENTIMENT: BLANK

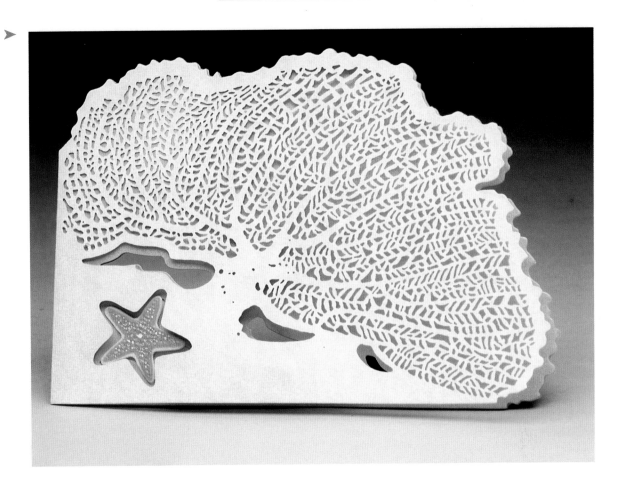

PUBLISHER
Current Inc./Best Kept Secrets
ART DIRECTOR
Catherine Alvord
ARTIST/ILLUSTRATOR
Brenda Walton

This card is die cut so a personal photograph can be inserted to create a memorable gift.

PUBLISHER
Outreach Publications
ARTIST/ILLUSTRATOR
Jim Needham/Product Concept, Inc.

This Christmas card is also a puzzle.

PUBLISHER
Current, Inc.

This charming Christmas card doubles as an advent calendar. Each door is numbered and meant to be opened, starting with December 1st and leading up to the 25th day of December—Christmas.

PUBLISHER
Old Print Factory

Reproduced from a turn-of-the-century antique paper collection, this diminutive card offers a kitten button keepsake.

INSIDE SENTIMENT: BLANK

PUBLISHER
Cardtricks
ART DIRECTOR
**Simms Taback,
Reynold Ruffins**
ARTIST/ILLUSTRATOR
Reynold Ruffins

This die-cut cat card contains an elastic band so the recipient can wear it as a mask.

PUBLISHER
**The Great Northwestern
Greeting Seed Co.**
ARTIST/ILLUSTRATOR
Nancy Olson

A packet of hot chocolate is enclosed in this sweet get well card.

Louie Awards

The Louie Awards were started in 1988 to showcase the best cards the greeting card industry produced. Named after Louis Prang, the Father of the American Greeting Card, they have brought much well deserved attention and excitement to the many creative talents in the industry.

Sponsored by the Greeting Card Association, publishers are invited to submit cards in the following categories: Anniversary, Birthday-Humorous, Birthday-Juvenile, Birthday-Traditional, New Baby, Blank Occasion, Blank Non-Occasion, Business-to-Business, Christmas-Humorous, Christmas-Religious, Christmas-Traditional, Easter, Father's Day, Friendship-Humorous, Friendship-Traditional, Foreign Language, Graduation, Get Well-Humorous, Get Well-Traditional, Halloween, Jewish Holidays, Mother's Day, Romantic Love, Special Occasion, Sympathy, Thanksgiving, Valentine's Day-Humorous, Valentine's Day-Juvenile, and Valentine's Day-Traditional. Each category is subdivided into two parts: "Above $2.00" and "$2.00 and Below."

The deadline for submissions is in December, the judging takes place in February, and the winners are announced at a dinner dance held in May on the opening night of the New York Stationery Show. Although the Louie Awards are still in their infancy, they have resulted in recognition of the greeting card industry's many contributions to American communication.

PUBLISHER
Old Print Factory

The images on this beautiful 1991 Louie Award nominee were reproduced from a turn-of-the-century paper collection. More than just a card, it's a working fan.

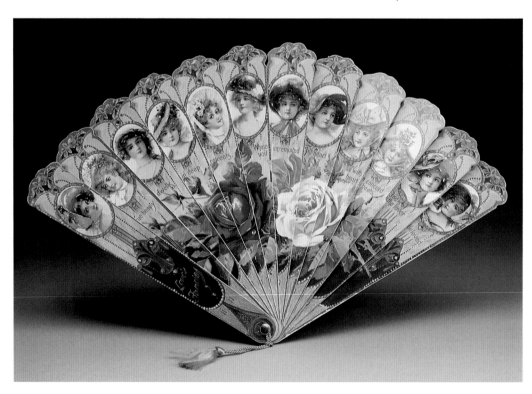

PUBLISHER
The Gifted Line, John Grossman, Inc.
ART DIRECTOR
Deborah Patterson
ARTIST/ILLUSTRATOR
Unknown, c. 1895. From the John Grossman collection of Antique

This diminutive 1990 Louie Award nominee is beautifully illustrated, subtly colored and features an unusual die-cut fold.

INSIDE SENTIMENT: BLANK

PUBLISHER
Linda Jade Charles
PHOTOGRAPHER
Kenneth Gregg

The gold frame of this 1991 Louie Award Winner is heavily embossed and decorated. Gold cords are attached to simulate a hanging picture.

INSIDE SENTIMENT: BLANK

PUBLISHER
Current, Inc.
ART DIRECTOR
Merrily Johnson
ARTIST/ILLUSTRATOR
R. Dean Grist
EDITORIAL
Nan Roloff

This textured card is elaborately embossed and delicately printed in beautiful pastels on textured stock.

INSIDE SENTIMENT:

You bring out the smiles in me!

PUBLISHER
Success, a division of Gibson Greetings, Inc.

This beautifully die-cut tri-fold is enhanced with embossing and pearlized foil. This card was nominated for a 1990 Louie Award in the Foreign Language category.

PARA SU *Aniversario De Bodas*

Ustedes forman una pareja muy especial y se merecen un mundo de felicidad.

Felicitaciones y los mejores deseos al celebrar su aniversario.

PUBLISHER
Paper House Productions
ART DIRECTOR
Jeffrey Milstein
PHOTOGRAPHER
Jeffrey Milstein

This photographic, die-cut birthday card is diminutive, yet striking.

PUBLISHER
Pinx A Card Co., Inc.

A theme of world unity is carried out by the charming illustration, which is printed in full color on both sides of the card.

INSIDE SENTIMENT: BLANK

PUBLISHER
Dickens Company
ART DIRECTOR
Marilyn Conklyn

This delightful Spanish language Christmas card contains a musical computer chip, so that when it is opened the card plays "Feliz Navidad" and the Christmas lights on the reindeer's antlers and nose twinkle in time to the music.

PUBLISHER
Herlin Card, Div. of Graphics 3 Inc.

This Christmas house won the coveted "Card of the Year" award in 1990.

PUBLISHER
Paper D'Art

Charming teddy bears, printed on two sides, grace this extra-ordinary three-dimensional canopy card which actually spins around. This card won the industry's highest honor, when it was named "Card of the Year" at the 1991 Louie Award ceremony.

Gift Enclosures

A gift enclosure card is a small card that is attached in some way to a present. Martha Banning Thomas is commonly credited with having created the concept. In 1913 she sold a gift card sentiment she had written to a Boston publisher who marketed it successfully. Thanks to their combined efforts, the gift enclosure card, complete with verse, remained popular for several decades.

Over the years, the size of these cards has decreased; today the average gift enclosure card is smaller than a 2″ × 3½″ business card. Although lengthy sentiments are no longer pre-printed, the small size makes it easy for gift givers to write a short message inside.

The artwork on gift enclosure cards seldom employs words. Frequently, the design coordinates with the gift wrap or gift bag. Like greeting cards, some gift enclosure cards were produced using special treatments such as die-cutting or foil-stamping. Gift enclosure cards are less expensive than greeting cards which might explain their recent resurgence in popularity.

PUBLISHER
Christina Parrett, Inc.
ART DIRECTOR
Christina Parrett
ARTIST/ILLUSTRATOR
Christina Parrett

PUBLISHER
Paper House Productions
ART DIRECTOR
Jeffrey Milstein
PHOTOGRAPHER
Jeffrey Milstein

PUBLISHER
Clearwater Graphics, Inc.
ART DIRECTOR
Sandy Gullikson
ARTIST/ILLUSTRATOR
Sandy Gullikson

PUBLISHER
Carole Smith Gallery Inc.
ARTIST/ILLUSTRATOR
Barbara Macomber

PUBLISHER
Faux Designs
ARTIST/ILLUSTRATOR
Stacy Landau

PUBLISHER
**Marian Heath Greeting
Cards Inc.**

PUBLISHER
**Carole Smith Gallery
Inc.**
ARTIST/ILLUSTRATOR
Donald Ewen

PUBLISHER
**The Gifted Line, John
Grossman, Inc.**

PUBLISHER
**Star of David Greeting
Cards**
ARTIST/ILLUSTRATOR
Jacqueline Tuteur

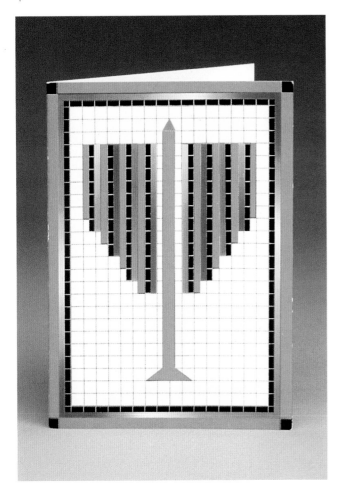

PUBLISHER
Elizabeth Lucas Designs
ART DIRECTOR
Elizabeth Lucas
ARTIST/ILLUSTRATOR
Elizabeth Lucas

PUBLISHER
Elizabeth Lucas Designs
ART DIRECTOR
Elizabeth Lucas
ARTIST/ILLUSTRATOR
Elizabeth Lucas

PUBLISHER
Colors by Design
ART DIRECTOR
Tamara Harrell
ARTIST/ILLUSTRATOR
Stephen Davis

PUBLISHER
Paper House Productions
ART DIRECTOR
Jeffrey Milstein
PHOTOGRAPHER
Jeffrey Milstein

PUBLISHER
Paper House Productions
ART DIRECTOR
Jeffrey Milstein
PHOTOGRAPHER
Jeffrey Milstein

PUBLISHER
Paper House Productions
ART DIRECTOR
Jeffrey Milstein
PHOTOGRAPHER
Jeffrey Milstein

PUBLISHER
Meri Meri
ART DIRECTOR
Meredithe D'Arcy

PUBLISHER
**Marcel Schurman
Company, Inc.**

PUBLISHER
Curtis Swann

PUBLISHER
Meri Meri
ART DIRECTOR
Meredithe D'Arcy

Handmade

Hand-crafted cards have been around for centuries. Despite the popularity of commercially published cards, many people enjoy creating something unique to send to someone special. These cards vary from amateurish endeavors to miniature pieces of fine art. Most hand-crafted cards are one-of-a-kind works created by talented artists or craftspeople. As public awareness and interest has grown, some enterprising artists have started cottage industry businesses to sell their designs. Hand-crafted cards are quite labor intensive and therefore tend to be more expensive than most printed cards. Despite the price, consumers have made hand-crafted cards a growing niche in the market. Frequently the cards are purchased not just to send, but to frame as well.

ARTIST/ILLUSTRATOR
Mary Worthington

This specially hand-constructed card utilizes oriental wrapping paper glued to heavy linen stock, textured stock for the insert, and a lovely red satin ribbon to tie it all together.

◄ PUBLISHER
Fan Mail Greeting Card Co.
ARTIST/ILLUSTRATOR
Dona Rozanski

This accordion-folded heart appliqué is strewn with thread decorations and swirls of color.

◄ ARTIST/ILLUSTRATOR
Connie Kreuzer

This extraordinary card uses pressed flowers affixed to a handmade paper heart which is glued onto a folded sheet of handmade paper. Seed pearls were later adhered to the card as a delightful finishing touch.

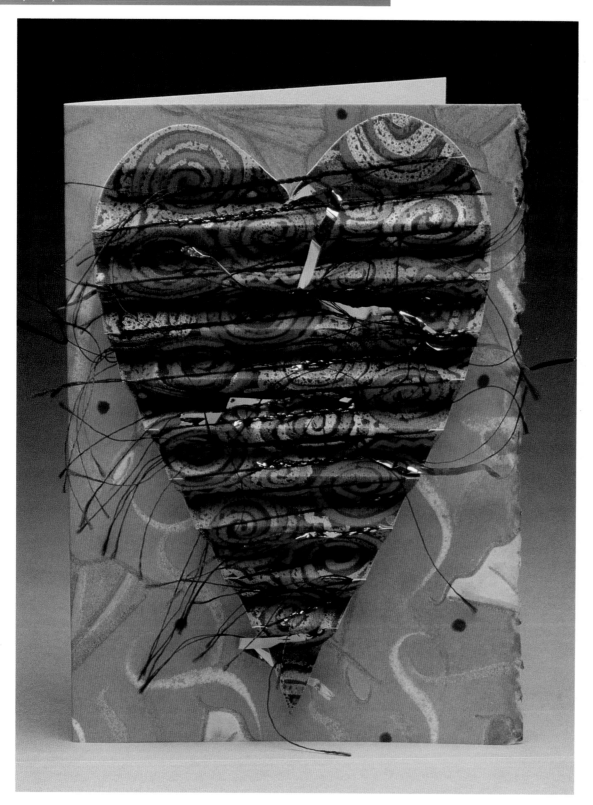

PUBLISHER
Fan Mail Greeting Card Co.
ARTIST/ILLUSTRATOR
Dona Rozanski

The bold contemporary patterning of this accordion fold heart is set against a softer colored background.

INSIDE SENTIMENT: BLANK

ARTIST/ILLUSTRATOR
Diana Stetson
COMPANY OWNER/
ARTIST REPRESENTATIVE
Constance Kay

This hand constructed card contains an interesting collage which features a U.S. postage stamp as a primary design element.

INSIDE SENTIMENT: BLANK

ARTIST/ILLUSTRATOR
Suze Weinberg

This card was created with decorative rubber stamps from "Stampa Barbara."

"Pagoda"   J.Lewis

PUBLISHER
Jack Lewis
ART DIRECTOR
Suzi Lewis
ARTIST/ILLUSTRATOR
Suzi Lewis

This striking geometric design was hand painted and then appliquéd onto a textured backing.

INSIDE SENTIMENT: BLANK

ARTIST/ILLUSTRATOR
Judy Kastin

This elegant illustration was hand painted on oriental rice paper and then adhered to a glossy, speckletone card-stock base.

INSIDE SENTIMENT: BLANK

◄ ARTIST/ILLUSTRATOR
Judy Kastin

This lovely illustration of bamboo was hand painted with watercolor and touches of pearlized paint.

INSIDE SENTIMENT: BLANK

PUBLISHER
Meri Meri
ART DIRECTOR
Meredithe D'Arcy
ARTIST/ILLUSTRATOR
Meredithe D'Arcy

►

The embossed pattern on this snake helps create a vivid, realistic image.

INSIDE SENTIMENT: BLANK

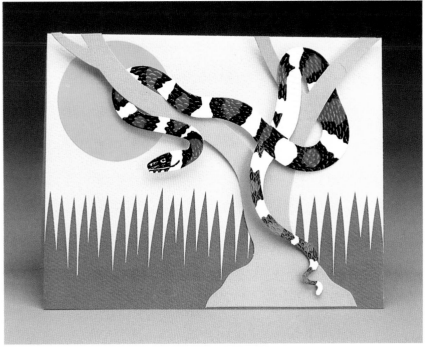

PUBLISHER
Linda Jade Charles

This wonderful group of handmade cards features beautifully printed Japanese papers, which are hand folded into shapes of different kimonos.

INSIDE SENTIMENT: BLANK

PUBLISHER
Linda Jade Charles

These shirt cards feature hand applied touches such as a string of pearls or an embroidered tie. The front flap of each card opens by folding down from underneath the collar. There is a white sheet tipped inside for message writing.

PUBLISHER
Mary Belshaw

A simple ink drawing of a peace dove adorns the front of this Christmas card.

INSIDE SENTIMENT: BLANK

ARTIST/ILLUSTRATOR
Merida Burkhart

This outstanding booklet card contains an appliquéd marbelized paper bow. When opened, it reveals hand-lettered Season's Greetings in a number of different languages.

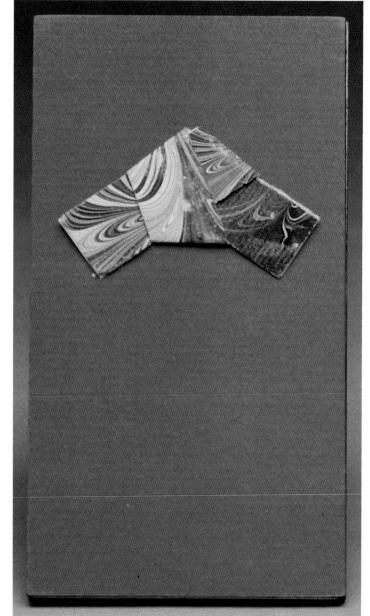

PUBLISHER
Lydia's Land

Torn paper hearts were glued onto this hand-lettered card to add color and impact.

INSIDE SENTIMENT: BLANK

ARTIST/ILLUSTRATOR
Gay Ayers

This colorful collage features calligraphy, printed music, handmade paper, sequins and a Christmas postage stamp.

INSIDE SENTIMENT: BLANK

ARTIST/ILLUSTRATOR
Paula Brinkman

This series of hand-painted vegetable/fruit cards was selected for its vibrant colors and wonderful illustrative techniques.

INSIDE SENTIMENT: BLANK

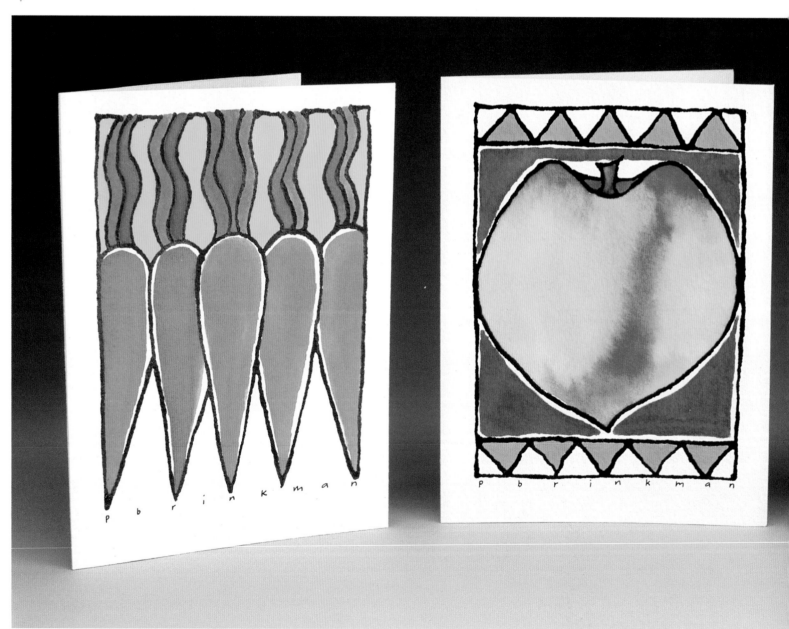

I Love You!

▲

ARTIST/ILLUSTRATOR
Paula Brinkman

Bright colors combined with bold graphics make this hand painted card so delightful.

INSIDE SENTIMENT: BLANK

ART DIRECTOR
Joanne Fink
ARTIST/ PAPERMAKER
Judy Mueller

Layers of handmade paper form this delicate scenic image.

INSIDE SENTIMENT: BLANK

ARTIST/ PAPERMAKER
Judy Mueller

This sailboat scene is a collage created from small pieces of handmade paper.

INSIDE SENTIMENT: BLANK

ARTIST/ILLUSTRATOR
Mary Worthington

This handmade paper collage is striking against a heavy blue paper backing. The thread appliqué adds a lovely touch.

INSIDE SENTIMENT: BLANK

Publishers

Art Directors

INDEX

Artists/Illustrators